ARCO

Clear and Simple Guide to Bookkeeping

Barbara Gilder Quint

MANAGEMENT INSTITUTE, NEW YORK UNIVERSITY

Money Management Editor, GLAMOUR AND FAMILY CIRCLE MAGAZINES

Prentice Hall
New York • London • Toronto • Sydney • Tokyo • Singapore

First Edition
Original title: *First Year Bookkeeping*

Prentice Hall General Reference
15 Columbus Circle
New York, NY 10023

An Arco Book

ISBN: 0-671-42108-5

Manufactured in the United States of America

15   16   17   18   19   20

Contents

Introduction

Today, many people have an increasing need to learn more about the nuts and bolts of keeping financial records. For some, it reflects a desire to maintain better personal money management records. For others, however, it's a key step to progress on the job. This progress may involve actually becoming a bookkeeper or adding bookkeeping functions to the other work you are doing at your company. Or it may mean learning more about the methods a business uses to keep track of its activities, even if you never actually take on many specific bookkeeping functions. In any event, bookkeeping is the language of business, and regardless of the actual tasks you do now at your present job, if you want to get ahead, you will need the overview that only a knowledge of bookkeeping procedures and terms can give you.

This book offers a step by step guide to bookkeeping, explaining each procedure carefully and without unnecessary jargon, along with many clear and relevant examples. We'll show you exactly what you need to know each step of the way, and at the end of each section, there's a set of questions, with answers, so that you can be sure you've understood the material.

Whether you are an absolute beginner, or someone with knowledge of the field who wants a handy reference book to consult when a question arises, you will find this book an invaluable guide to the bookkeeping practices now in general use in the business world.

Barbara Gilder Quint
New York, 1981

Nature of Bookkeeping | 1

IMPORTANCE OF BOOKKEEPING

The study of bookkeeping can be important to the student in various ways:

1. **As a Citizen.** Bookkeeping terms and ideas are used to express many of the activities that citizens engage in every day. A knowledge of bookkeeping will therefore help us to understand how business works and its role in our society.
2. **As a Consumer.** With some knowledge of the principles of bookkeeping, an individual is better prepared to keep his own personal financial records. He will also have the information needed to make sensible decisions in regard to such things as borrowing money, handling checking accounts, paying personal bills, etc. Personal bookkeeping and record keeping are also important as a help in preparing personal income tax returns.
3. **As a Wage Earner.** Some students will actually become bookkeepers, and help in keeping the records of a business. A knowledge of bookkeeping will prove very helpful, however, to other business workers too. It will give them a broad understanding of the general nature of business operations. With this kind of understanding, it is possible to do one's own specific job as a typist, clerk, secretary or junior executive in a more intelligent manner. In addition, a person is more likely to be considered for promotion to a better position in his own field if he has this broader understanding of total business operations that a knowledge of bookkeeping provides.
4. **As a Businessman.** The small businessman finds it hard to run a business if all he knows is his own particular trade.
   a. NEED FOR RECORDS FOR GOVERNMENT. Today, every businessman is legally responsible to the government for record keeping in connection with such things as social security taxes, withholding of income taxes and sales taxes, etc.
   b. NEED FOR RECORDS IN ORDER TO OPERATE PROFITABLY. A businessman must keep good records in order to make sure that he pays his bills, and that he collects bills that others owe him. Adequate record keeping is also necessary to the businessman so that he can be sure he is charging prices that will net him a profit. In other words, a basic knowledge of bookkeeping is needed in order to operate a small business efficiently.

DUTIES OF A BOOKKEEPER

The specific duties of a bookkeeper in a business firm or other organization will vary from one business to another. In general, the bookkeeper is responsible for recording the transactions that take place in connection with a business operation. In a small firm, he may be responsible for keeping all the records; in a larger company he may handle transactions in only one area.

CHARACTERISTICS OF THE BOOKKEEPER

A good bookkeeper will have several important characteristics:

1. **Neatness.** Neat work is less likely to have mistakes. It is also easier for another person to read and understand when he wishes to consult the records.
2. **Accuracy.** Inaccurate records can be very costly. For example, if the record of money owed by customers to a firm is not right, these customers may never be billed, and the firm may never collect the money.
3. **Ability to Keep His Work Up to Date.** Bookkeeping records are of much more use to a business if they are up-to-date and can therefore provide the latest possible picture of the business's operations.
4. **Understanding of His Job, Rather Than Memorization of Certain Rules.** The good bookkeeper will understand the meaning and significance of everything he does, instead of just following rules mechanically.

1

Assets, Liabilities and Proprietorship | 2

ASSETS

Assets are anything of value that is owned.

1. **Personal Assets.** Personal assets include such things as a house, a car, a typewriter or cash owned by an individual.
2. **Business Assets.** Business assets are those things that a business owns—cash in the bank or the cash register, desks and filing cabinets, stationery and other office supplies, factories, merchandise that the business hopes to sell, etc. Another business asset is unpaid bills of customers for goods sold on credit. These unpaid bills of customers for merchandise bought on account are called *accounts receivable*.

LIABILITIES

Liabilities are debts. Those who lend money are called *creditors*, and the amounts of money owed to them are called *liabilities*.

1. **Personal Liabilities.** Typical liabilities of an individual are debts owed to a bank, a loan company or department store. Money might be owed to a bank in connection with the purchase of an automobile. Money might be owed to a department store because clothing was bought and charged.
2. **Business Liabilities.** Typical liabilities of a business are debts owed to a manufacturer for merchandise shipped on credit, or funds owed to a bank which has loaned the business money. Bills which a business *owes* for items *bought on credit* are called *accounts payable*.

PROPRIETORSHIP

Proprietorship is that part of the assets which belongs to the owners, after subtracting the claims of the creditors. For example, Mr. Howard has a car worth $6,000. He took a loan of $1,500 from the bank to purchase the car. That part of the car that he owns is $4,500. This is called his *proprietorship interest*. Proprietorship is also called by other names: capital, ownership equity, owner's equity, or net worth.

Relationship Between Assets, Liabilities and Proprietorship—the Fundamental Accounting Equation

3

FUNDAMENTAL ACCOUNTING EQUATION

Assets can be acquired with funds supplied either by owners or by creditors. Therefore, owners and/ or creditors will have certain rights or claims against those assets for which they have provided the funds to buy. The *fundamental accounting equation* (also called *fundamental bookkeeping equation*) states that the value of the assets must always equal the value of the rights of the creditors plus the rights of the owners.

1. **Assets = Liabilities + Proprietorship.** Mr. Howard's car (his asset) is worth $6,000. The bank (creditor) has a claim of $1,500 against it. Mr. Howard's interest in the car (proprietorship) is $4,500.

Value of assets	=	Creditor's interest	+	Proprietorship interest
$6,000	=	$1,500	+	$4,500

or, to phrase it another way:

$$\text{Assets} = \text{Liabilities} + \text{Proprietorship.}$$

2. **Assets − Liabilities = Proprietorship.** There is another way of stating this fundamental accounting equation. We can see that the owner's interest or rights to an asset will equal the value of the asset, less any debts owed.

$$\text{Proprietorship} = \text{Assets} - \text{Liabilities}$$

Mr. Howard's car is worth $6,000 and a debt of $1,500 is owed against it. The value of the car less the debt will equal Mr. Howard's proprietorship interest in it.

Proprietorship	=	Assets	−	Liabilities
$4,500	=	$6,000	−	$1,500

BALANCE SHEET

One of the simplest ways of showing the assets, liabilities and proprietorship of an individual or a business is in a *balance sheet*.

1. **Definition.** A balance sheet is a listing of the assets as of a certain date, and of the claims

against these assets as of that date—the liabilities and the proprietorship. For example, if we assume that all Mr. Howard owned and owed on Sept. 1, 1960, was his automobile and his bank loan, a very simple balance sheet for him might be drawn up.

Assets	Liabilities and Proprietorship
Automobile $6,000	Bank Loan $1,500 Mr. Howard's proprietorship interest $4,500

2. **Form of the Balance Sheet.** When an actual balance sheet for an individual or a business is prepared, certain definite procedures are followed. (The form shown here is the *"Account form."* Another form of balance sheet—the report form—is illustrated in Chapter 28.)

   a. HEADING.

   (1) NAME. The name of the individual or business firm is placed on the first line in the center of the page.

   (2) TITLE. The title, *Balance Sheet*, is on the second line.

   (3) DATE. The date as of which the figures are given is listed on the third line.

   b. LEFT-HAND SIDE. The assets are listed on the left. A column heading, "Assets," is centered above the individual items. The name of each asset and its dollar value is listed.

   c. RIGHT-HAND SIDE. The claims against assets appear on the right-hand side. There are two kinds of claims—liabilities and proprietorship—so the right-hand side is divided into two sections.

   (1) LIABILITIES. A column heading, "Liabilities," is centered above the individual liability items, and then the name of each liability and its dollar value is listed.

   (2) PROPRIETORSHIP. A column heading, "Proprietorship," is centered above the name of the holder of the ownership or proprietorship interest.

   d. TOTALS. After the dollar value of each asset has been listed, a single line is ruled to show that a total follows. After the total amount of assets is written, a *double* line is drawn to show *the end of the statement.* Similar procedures are followed for the right-hand side. A single line is drawn under the listing of all dollar amounts of liabilities, and they are totaled. Then a single line is drawn under the amount of the *proprietorship.* Total liabilities and total proprietorship are then added together, and a double line is drawn underneath this total to show the end of the statement. The two totals—1) Total Assets and 2) Total Liabilities and Proprietorship—should appear on same line.

e. TOTAL ASSETS = TOTAL LIABILITIES + TOTAL PPROPRIETORSHIP. In every balance sheet, the fundamental accounting equation will hold true. The dollar value of the assets listed on the left-hand side must always equal the dollar value of the creditors' plus owners claims against these assets. In other words, both sides of the balance sheet must always be equal.

SWEET CANDY STORE
Balance Sheet
December 31, 198–

Assets		Liabilities	
Cash	5,000.00	Bon Ton Supply Co.	2,000.00
Inventory	10,000.00	Delicious Corp.	5,000.00
Store Fixtures	5,000.00	Total Liabilities	7,000.00
		Proprietorship	
		Robert Brown, Capital	13,000.00
Total Assets	20,000.00	Total Liabilities & Prop.	20,000.00

EFFECT OF BUSINESS TRANSACTIONS ON FUNDAMENTAL ACCOUNTING EQUATION

Every time a business transaction takes place, changes will also take place in some of the items that make up the balance sheet or the fundamental accounting equation. We know that both sides of the equation must always remain equal. Therefore, it is clear that any additions or subtractions to one item *must also involve changes in another item.* Thus, there are two important facts to remember about every business transaction:

1. **Each Transaction Ultimately Affects at Least 2 Balance Sheet Items** (or their components).
2. **At The Conclusion of Each Transaction, Both Sides of the Accounting Equation (and of the balance sheet) Must Be Equal.**

EXAMPLE 1: The Green Company has cash of $10,000 and merchandise of $20,000. It owes the bank $5,000, and Mr. Green's proprietorship interest in the business is $25,000. A simple balance sheet for Green Co. might look like this.

GREEN COMPANY

Cash	$10,000	Bank Loan	$ 5,000
Merchandise	20,000	Mr. Green, Capital	$25,000

At this point, the fundamental accounting equation for Green Co. would show that:

$$\text{Assets} = \text{Liabilities} + \text{Proprietorship}$$
$$\$30,000 = \$5,000 + \$25,000$$

Assume that Mr. Green borrows an additional $5,000 from the bank and gets cash. This would affect the balance sheet and the fundamental accounting equation in 2 areas: 1) cash would increase by $5,000; 2) bank loan would increase by $5,000.

At the conclusion of the transaction, both sides of the equation are again equal:

$$\text{Assets} = \text{Liabilities} + \text{Proprietorship}$$
$$\$30,000 + \text{additional } \$5,000 = (\$5,000 + \text{additional } \$5,000) + \$25,000$$

EXAMPLE 2: It is not necessary for a business transaction to increase both sides of the fundamental accounting equation, as it did in the preceding example. Sometimes, one asset is exchanged for another. For example, Mr. Jones has $10,000 in cash, of which $4,000 is his own money and $6,000 was obtained from a bank loan. His fundamental accounting equation would read:

$$\text{Assets} = \text{Liabilities} + \text{Proprietorship}$$
$$\$10,000 = \$6,000 + \$4,000$$

He uses $500 of his cash to buy a typewriter. The new fundamental accounting equation would read:

$$\$9,500 + \$500 = \$6,000 + \$4,000$$
$$\text{Cash} + \text{Typewriter} = \text{Bank loan} + \text{Proprietorship}$$

The totals are the same, but the composition of the assets has changed.

Income and Expense | 4

INCOME

A business firm sells merchandise or services. The proceeds of these sales are called *income*. The income in a manufacturing business or a store comes mostly from *sales*. The income in a service business or a profession comes mostly from *fees* for services performed. There are also other forms of income. For example, interest paid by a bank on a savings account is called *interest income*.

EXPENSE

Any payments that are made in connection with producing income are called expenses. Rent, electricity, salaries of employees, advertising, etc., are typical expenses.

PROFIT OR LOSS

If income received during a period of time is larger than expenses, the business will have a *profit*. If expenses exceed income, a *loss* will result.

EFFECT OF INCOME AND EXPENSES ON PROPRIETORSHIP

Every time income is received, the ownership interest in the business—the proprietorship—is increased. Every expense decreases proprietorship. If, at the end of a period of time, income has exceeded expense, the profit that results belongs to the owners, and the ownership interest has been increased. In other words, the proprietorship interest at the end of the period will be equal to the original proprietorship plus profit. If the fundamental equation at the beginning is expressed as

$$Assets \ = \ Liabilities \ + \ Proprietorship,$$

then the equation at the end of a period of business can be expressed as

$$Assets = Liabilities + Original\ Proprietorship + Profit\ or - Loss.$$
$$or$$
$$Assets = Liabilities + Original\ Requisition + (Income - Expense).$$

EXAMPLE 1: Mr. Jones, a lawyer, starts in practice with $8,000 of office equipment, a $2,000 bank loan *and* $6,000 of proprietorship or ownership in his business.

Assets	Liabilities
$8,000 Office Equipment	$2,000 Bank Loan
	Proprietorship
	$6,000 Mr. Jones, Capital

During the month he collects $5,000 in fees and spends $2,000 in rent and other expenses. At the end of the month he has:

Assets	Liabilities
$3,000 Cash	$2,000 Bank Loan
$8,000 Office Equipment	**Proprietorship**
	$6,000 Original Proprietorship
	$3,000 Profit

The fundamental equation could therefore be expressed as:

$$Assets = Liabilities + Original\ Proprietorship + Income - Expenses$$
$$\$11,000 = \$2,000 + \$6,000 + \$5,000 - \$2,000$$

5

Use of Accounts 5

DIRECT BALANCE SHEET ACCOUNTING

We have seen how each business transaction affects at least two balance sheet items or their components. Theoretically, it would be possible to show the effect of each business transaction by showing its effect directly on the balance sheet accounts. This is called *direct balance sheet accounting* and involves drawing up a new balance sheet after each transaction.

EXAMPLE 1: Mr. Jones' March 1 balance sheet shows the following:

Assets		Liabilities	
Cash	$500	Owed to auto dealer	$3,000
Car	$6,000		

	Proprietorship	
	Mr. Jones, Capital	$3,500

On March 2, Mr. Jones pays the auto dealer $300, reducing his loan to $2,700. We could show this by drawing up a new balance sheet.

Assets		Liabilities	
Cash	$200	Owed to auto dealer	$2,700
Car	$6,000		

	Proprietorship	
	Mr. Jones, Capital	$3,500

1. **Limitations of Direct Balance Sheet Accounting.** Direct balance sheet accounting is cumbersome and time consuming, especially for businesses where there are many transactions each day.

USE OF A SYSTEM OF ACCOUNTS

The simplest way of keeping track of the effect of transactions is through a system of *accounts*. A record of all the transactions that affect each balance sheet item is kept together. This record is called the *account*. For example, records of all transactions involving cash are kept in the *cash account*.

FORM OF AN ACCOUNT

The form of an account (usually called a T account because of its basic shape) involves three parts.
1. **Title.** This is the name of the item which is affected by the transactions recorded in the account. For example, all increases and decreases in cash will be recorded in the cash account.
2. **Left Side.** The left side of the account is called the debit side.
3. **Right Side.** The right side of the account is called the credit side.

EXAMPLE 2:

Cash Account

Debit side	Credit side

USE OF TERMS DEBIT AND CREDIT

The terms debit and credit have special meanings when used in bookkeeping.
1. **Debit.** In bookkeeping, debit refers to any amount recorded in the *left*-hand side of an account. When an amount is recorded in the left-hand side of an account, the account is said to be *debited* or *charged*. *Dr.* is the abbreviation for debit.
2. **Credit.** In bookkeeping, credit refers to any amount recorded in the right-hand side of an account. Crediting an account means entering an amount in the right-hand side. *Cr.* is the abbreviation for credit.

EXAMPLE 3:

Cash Account

(a) $100	$50 (b)

Item (a) shows a *debit* of $100 to the cash account (on left side).
Item (b) shows a *credit* of $50 to the cash account (on right side).

RULES FOR DEBITING AND CREDITING ACCOUNTS

It is very important to learn the rules by which the different kinds of accounts are debited and credited. These rules are stated briefly here, and are explained again with more examples in Chapter 6 which explains the Ledger.

1. **Asset Accounts.** We have seen that assets are listed on the left-hand side of the balance sheet. The following will help you to remember the rules for asset accounts.

Balance Sheet

Assets	Liabilities
	Proprietorship
Left	Right

a. INCREASES IN ASSETS ARE LISTED ON THE LEFT-HAND SIDE OF ACCOUNT. An increase in an asset is recorded by debiting the asset account (increasing the left-hand side).

b. DECREASES IN ASSETS ARE LISTED ON THE RIGHT-HAND SIDE OF ACCOUNT. A decrease in an asset is shown in the asset account by crediting the account (increasing the right-hand side).

EXAMPLE 4:

Cash Account

(a) $500	$200 (b)

Entry (a) on the left above for $500 shows that an increase of $500 has taken place in cash. This is shown by *debiting* the account. Entry (b), a *credit* of $200, shows that a payout or withdrawal or reduction of cash has occurred.

2. **Liability Accounts.** Liability accounts are listed on the *right-hand* side of the balance sheet. This may help you to remember the rule that increases in liability accounts are shown on the right side of the account.

a. INCREASES IN LIABILITY ACCOUNTS ARE LISTED ON THE RIGHT-HAND SIDE. An increase in a liability is shown by crediting the liability account, that is, entering the amount on the right-hand side.

b. DECREASES IN LIABILITY ACCOUNTS ARE LISTED ON THE LEFT-HAND SIDE. A decrease in a liability is shown by recording the amount on the left-hand side of the account, that is, by *debiting* the account.

EXAMPLE 5:

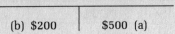

Bank Loan Account (Notes Payable)

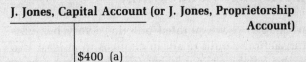

(b) $200	$500 (a)

Entry (a) on the right side is a *credit* to the notes payable account. It records an increase in the amount of bank loans the firm had. When the firm paid off $200 of its bank loan, and the bank loan was reduced, this *decrease* in a liability was shown by a *debit* entry on the left-hand side of the account (b).

3. **Proprietorship Accounts.** Proprietorship accounts (which also appear on the right-hand side of the balance sheet account along with the liability accounts) are debited and credited just as liability accounts are.

a. INCREASES IN PROPRIETORSHIP ACCOUNTS ARE LISTED ON THE RIGHT-HAND SIDE. An increase in a proprietorship account is shown by a credit entry on the right-hand side of the account.

b. DECREASES IN PROPRIETORSHIP ACCOUNTS ARE SHOWN ON THE LEFT-HAND SIDE. A reduction in a *proprietorship* account is shown by a debit entry on the left-hand side of the account.

EXAMPLE 6:

J. Jones, Capital Account (or J. Jones, Proprietorship Account)

	$400 (a)

Entry (a) above is a credit to the proprietorship account. It shows an increase in the account.

4. **Income Accounts.** We saw in Chapter 4 how income increased proprietorship and expenses decreased proprietorship. We could show each income transaction by increasing the proprietorship account directly. In other words, every time there was a sale and income was produced, we could show an increase in the proprietorship account by crediting the proprietorship account.

Instead of recording each amount of income directly as a credit to the proprietorship account, bookkeepers keep separate records of income in separate accounts. These are called *income accounts*.

We have said that *income increases proprietorship*, and would therefore be recorded on the *right* or *credit* side of the proprietorship account. When we list income in its own individual income account, the same procedure is followed. Income is recorded on the right or *credit* side of the *income account*.

EXAMPLE 7: The Jones Company has sales of $10,000. We wish to show this sales income in its own account. To do this, the sales income account is credited with $10,000.

Sales Income

$10,000 (a) |

5. Expense Accounts. Expenses decrease the proprietorship account, and might therefore be listed directly in the proprietorship account by debits in the left-hand side. (We know that decreases in proprietorship accounts are shown by debits.) Instead, however, we keep separate expense accounts.

Expenses Are Recorded As Debits On The Left-Hand Side Of The Expense Account.

EXAMPLE 8: The Jones Company had $1,000 of rent expense during the month. We show this by a debit to the rent expense account.

Rent Expense

(a) $1,000 |

6. Summary of How Changes in Accounts Are Recorded.

Assets	Increases — Debits Decreases — Credits
Expenses	Expenses are recorded as debits in the expense account.

Liabilities —	Increases — Credits Decreases — Debits
Proprietorship —	Increases — Credits Decreases — Debits
Income —	Income is recorded as a credit to the income account.

DEBITING AND CREDITING OF ACCOUNTS AFTER EACH TRANSACTION

In Chapter 3 we pointed out that every business transaction would result in changes in at least two of the balance sheet items (or their components: expenses + income). In this chapter, we have seen how *accounts* are used to record these changes, rather than the balance sheet itself. Therefore, every time a transaction takes place, *at least two accounts will be affected.* We will record these transactions in the accounts by debiting and crediting the accounts. *Each transaction will result in equal debits and equal credits.*

1. **Procedure in Analyzing Transactions.** The following are the steps to follow in analyzing each business transaction to determine which accounts to debit and which accounts to credit:
   a. DECIDE WHICH ACCOUNTS ARE AFFECTED BY THE TRANSACTION. Determine which items have been increased or decreased, or whether income has been earned or expenses incurred.
   b. DEBIT AND CREDIT ACCORDING TO RULES. Determine whether to debit or credit the accounts in accordance with the rules you have learned.
   c. BE SURE DEBITS AND CREDITS FROM EACH TRANSACTION ARE EQUAL.

EXAMPLE 9: Jones Department store buys $3,000 worth of hats on credit from Gray Hat Company. What has happened? Jones' inventory of hats (merchandise) is *increased.* This is an *asset* account; to show an increase in an asset account, we debit the account. Therefore, merchandise account will be *debited* for $3,000. At the same time, the bills that Jones Company owes (its accounts payable) have also been *increased.* Accounts payable is a *liability* account; to show increase of a liability account, we credit the account. Therefore, accounts payable will be credited with $3,000.

EXAMPLE 10: Jones Department store buys $100 worth of office supplies and pays cash. Office supplies, an *asset*, has been *increased.* Show this increase by *debiting* the office supplies account with $100. Cash, an *asset*, has been *decreased.* Show this *decrease* of an asset by *crediting* the cash account for $100.

EXAMPLE 11: Mr. Jones, the owner of the company, takes $100 in cash out of the business. Since Mr. Jones took money out of the business, his ownership or proprietorship interest in it is *decreased.* Show this decrease in proprietorship by *debiting* the proprietorship account. Cash, an *asset*, has decreased. Show this *decrease* as an asset by crediting the cash account.

EXAMPLE 12: Jones Company pays rent of $1,000 in cash. An expense, rent, has been incurred. Show this *expense* by *debiting* the expense account, rent expense. Cash has been *reduced*. Show this decrease in an asset by *crediting* the cash account.

NOTE: In each case, debits and credits from each transaction are equal.

A. Identify each of the following as an *asset*, *liability* or *proprietorship* item.

   1. Cash in the bank.
   2. Cash in the cash register.
   3. Money owed to suppliers.
   4. Money owed to the bank.
   5. Accounts payable.
   6. Furniture and fixtures.
   7. Office supplies.
   8. Mr. Jones, capital account.
   9. Accounts receivable.
  10. Inventory.

B. Complete the sentence by choosing the correct answer from the given words or phrases.

   1. Another name for proprietorship account is

     a. Capital account.
     b. Accounts receivable.
     c. Accounts payable.
     d. Asset.

   2. Jones Broadcasting Company has assets of $5,000 and liabilities of $3,000. Proprietorship accounts must equal

     a. $8,000.
     b. $5,000.
     c. $3,000.
     d. $2,000.

   3. Robert Corporation has liabilities of $10,000 and proprietorship accounts of $8,000. Assets of the company are

     a. $2,000.
     b. $8,000.
     c. $10,000.
     d. $18,000.

   4. The right-hand side of the balance sheet consists of

     a. Assets.
     b. Liabilities.
     c. Assets and liabilities.
     d. Liabilities and proprietorship.

5. Every time income is earned

    a. A proprietorship account is increased.
    b. A proprietorship account is decreased.
    c. No effect on proprietorship account occurs.
    d. Liability account is increased.

6. In bookkeeping, crediting an account *always* means

    a. Increasing the account.
    b. Decreasing the account.
    c. Entering an amount on the left-hand side of the account.
    d. Entering an amount on the right-hand side of the account.

7. An increase in an asset is shown by

    a. Taking a trial balance.
    b. Crediting the account.
    c. Debiting the account.
    d. Entering the amount on the right-hand side.

8. Every business transaction

    a. Results in an increase of an asset.
    b. Results in equal debits and credits.
    c. Affects a liability and an asset account.
    d. Should be entered immediately in the balance sheet.

9. Another name for money owed to *suppliers* for merchandise shipped on credit is

    a. Accounts receivable.
    b. Assets.
    c. Accounts payable.
    d. Proprietorship.

10. Accounts receivable is

    a. An asset account.
    b. A liability account.
    c. A proprietorship account.
    d. An expense account.

C. Underline the correct answer.

1. An increase in an asset account is shown by a (debit, credit).
2. A decrease in a liability account is shown by a (debit, credit).
3. Expenses are recorded by (debiting, crediting) the expense account.
4. An increase in a proprietorship account is shown by a (debit, credit).
5. An increase in a liability account is shown by a (debit, credit).
6. A decrease in an asset account is shown by a (debit, credit).
7. Income is recorded by (debiting, crediting) the income account.
8. A decrease in cash is shown by (debiting, crediting) the cash account.
9. An increase in acccounts payable is shown by (debiting, crediting) the account.
10. When rent is paid, the rent expense account is (debited, credited).
11. When salaries are paid the *cash* account is (debited, credited).
12. When merchandise is bought on credit by a company, the accounts payable account is (debited, credited).
13. When a company pays a bill that was outstanding, its cash account is (debited, credited) and its accounts payable account is (debited, credited).

14. When a customer pays a bill that he owes the Jones Company, the Jones Company's cash is increased, and its accounts receivable are (increased, decreased).
15. When a customer pays a bill that he owes the Jones Company, the Jones Company's cash account should be (debited, credited) and its accounts receivable account should be (debited, credited).
16. When merchandise is sold for credit, the accounts receivable account is (increased, decreased) and this should be shown by (debiting, crediting) the accounts receivable.

D. Explain or identify:

1. Capital account.
2. Debit side of an account.
3. Liability account.
4. Fundamental accounting equation (or fundamental bookkeeping equation).
5. Balance sheet.

The Ledger | 6

THE LEDGER ACCOUNT

The actual form of the T account in which records are kept in a business is the "ledger account." A ledger account is a lined card or sheet of paper, divided into two sides and ruled into columns in order to simplify listing and adding of numbers. On each of the sides, spaces are provided to record the date, a brief description of the transaction, the amount of each entry in dollars and cents, and a posting reference column (explained later). There is a different ledger account kept for each balance sheet account, and for each of the income accounts and expense accounts that affect the proprietorship account.

Example of Ledger Sheet or Card

THE LEDGER

Groups of the individual ledger account cards or sheets are kept together and are called the *ledger*. They may be kept in a loose-leaf notebook, or in a filing drawer or cabinet.

THE CHART OF ACCOUNTS

A chart of accounts is prepared in order to help people find a particular ledger account in the ledger. Each account is given a number, the accounts are filed in the ledger in numerical order, and the chart of accounts shows the number which has been assigned to each account. Thus, the chart of accounts helps in finding a particular ledger account card or sheet when it is required, and in returning it to its proper place in the ledger afterwards.

Various systems for charts of accounts have been devised. A typical system provides that all *asset* accounts will have numbers in the 100's. *Liability* accounts will be numbered in the 200's, *proprietorship* accounts in the 300's, *income* accounts in the 400's and *expense* accounts in the 500's. Under such a system, the chart of accounts could look like this.

111	Cash
112	Accounts Receivable
113	Inventories
114	Fixtures
115	Office Equipment
211	Accounts Payable
212	Bank Loans Payable
311	John Jones, proprietorship account
411	Sales
511	Rent expense
512	Salary Expense

INITIAL ENTRIES IN LEDGER ACCOUNTS

When a new enterprise is started, ledger accounts are opened for each balance sheet item.

1. **Heading of Ledger Sheet.** Each ledger sheet is headed on the top line with the name of the

account, and its number, in accordance with the chart of accounts.

2. **Making the Opening Entry.** The right- or the left-hand side of the account will be used to list the amount, in accordance with the rules given in Chapter 5. *Assets are listed on the left or debit side of the asset account. Liabilities and proprietorship amounts are listed on the right or credit side of the account.*

   a. DATE COLUMN. The year is written in small numbers in the first date column, and the month is written beneath it. The date of the month is written in the second date column.

   b. ITEM COLUMN. (Also called account column.) The item (or account) column is used to explain the transaction that results in each entry in the ledger. In the case of opening or beginning accounts for balance sheet items, the word *"balance"* is written to show that this is a beginning or opening amount.

   c. POST. REF. COLUMN. Post. Ref. is the abbreviation for Posting Reference. This column is used to list the journal page on which the transaction was originally recorded, and serves as a cross reference. The journal is studied in Chapters 8 and 9, and the post. ref. column is explained there.

   d. AMOUNT COLUMN. The dollar amount of the item is entered here. Note that no dollar sign is used.

   e. EXAMPLES. The following two examples show initial entries for cash and proprietorship accounts. Note that cash, an asset, is recorded on the debit (left) side, and that proprietorship is listed on the credit (right) side. Liability accounts would also show opening balances on the credit (right) side.

INITIAL ENTRIES IN LEDGER

LEDGER ENTRIES RESULTING FROM TRANSACTIONS

During the course of business, various transactions will take place, and these must be recorded in the individual ledger accounts. The transaction will be listed on the right (credit) side or the left (debit) side of the account, in accordance with the rules given in Chapter 5.

DEBITS -   Asset increases
            Liability decreases
            Proprietorship decreases

            Expenses

CREDITS -   Asset decreases
            Liability increases
            Proprietorship increases

            Income

FORM OF LEDGER ENTRY

The form of each ledger entry is discussed in more detail in Chapters 10 to 12 under "posting." The following example shows how transactions are entered. The amount will be entered on the left-hand side if it is a debit; on the right-hand side if it is a credit. Note that the day of the month is entered for

13

each transaction, but the month and the year are entered *only when there is a change*. Explanations, if any, are entered in the item column. Post. Ref. refers to the journal (see Chapter 8), and the amount is listed in the last column.

DATE		ITEMS	POST REF	DEBIT	DATE		ITEMS	POST REF	CREDIT
198— Mar	1	Balance		500 00	*198—* Mar	2			200 00
	4			600 00					

Cash   Account #111

The above example of a cash ledger account shows an original balance-sheet item of $500 of cash. On March 4th, $600 more of cash was received and the account was debited. On March 2nd, $200 of cash was paid out and this entry is recorded as a credit.

(Note that the $600 increase of cash [an asset] is listed as a debit on the left-hand side of the account, and decreases of cash are listed as credits on the right-hand side.)

Trial Balance

USE OF TRIAL BALANCE

At intervals, one kind of check is made on the accuracy of the ledger accounts by preparing a *trial balance*. In most businesses this is usually done once a month. However, it may be done more or less often depending upon the needs of the business.

BALANCING EACH ACCOUNT

The first step in preparing a trial balance is to summarize the information *in each individual ledger account*.

1. **Footing the Account.** The bookkeeper takes an account and adds up each side of the account. First of all, the entries on the debit side are added, and the total is written in pencil in small numbers beneath the last number on the debit side. Then the same procedure is followed on the credit side. This is called *footing the*

account and the totals are called the *pencil footings*.

2. **Balancing the Account.**
   a. ACCOUNTS WITH ENTRIES ON ONLY ONE SIDE. Some accounts will have entries on only one side. For example, the sales account may have only credit entries. When this happens, the total on that one side (the footing) is the *balance in the account*.
   b. ACCOUNTS WITH ENTRIES ON TWO SIDES. Some accounts will have entries on both sides. For example, the cash account will have debit entries showing receipts of cash, and credit entries showing payouts of cash. After such an account has been footed, subtract the smaller side from the larger side, and write the difference underneath the explanation column of the larger side. This is called *balancing the account* and the number resulting from the subtraction is the *balance in the account*.

DATE	ITEMS	POST REF	DEBIT	DATE	ITEMS	POST REF	CREDIT
198– Mar 1	Balance		3 00 00	198– Mar 15			1 00 00
3			2 50 00	29			5 00 00
4			1 00 00				6 00 00
30			4 00 00				
	450.00		1 0 5 0 00				

Cash   Account #111

Footing and Balancing a Ledger Account

TRIAL BALANCE

The trial balance is *one* test of the accuracy of the ledger.

1. **Purpose.** Every time a business transaction occurs, equal debits and credits are supposed to be recorded in the ledger. Therefore, if the ledger has been kept correctly, *the total of all*

debit entries should equal *the total of all credit entries*. We can find this out by testing to see if the total of the debit balances of all the accounts equals the total of the credit balances.

2. **Method.** Prepare a listing of all the balances in all the ledger accounts. List the debit balances in one column and the credit balances in another. They should be equal. Such a listing is called a *trial balance*. If the debit and credit

columns are equal, the ledger is said to be *in balance*.

a. HEADING. At the top of the sheet, write the name of the business, the words "trial balance" and the date.

b. LIST OF LEDGER ACCOUNTS. Each ledger account with a balance is listed in the order in which it appears in the ledger. The number of the account is also given.

c. BALANCES. Debit balances are listed in the first column. Credit balances are listed in the second column.

d. TOTALING. Rule a single line under the last account balance. Add the two columns. If they are equal, draw a double line to show that the work has been completed and the trial balance is in balance. If the two columns are not equal, check for mistakes following the procedures listed below.

Barbara Banana Co.				
Trial Balance				
March 31, 198—				
Cash	111	450.00		
Accounts Receivable	121	200.00		
Inventory	131	500.00		
Office Supplies	141	100.00		
Accounts Payable	211		300.00	
J. Jones, capital	311		500.00	
Sales	411		650.00	
Rent Expense	511	100.00		
Miscellaneous Expense	512	100.00		
		1,450.00	1,450.00	

Trial Balance

UNBALANCED TRIAL BALANCE

When debit balances and credit balances are not equal, the trial balance is said to be *"out of balance."* There are several possible places where mistakes could have been made, and they should be investigated in the order given below.

1. **Addition of Trial Balance is Wrong.** Perhaps the actual addition of the debit or credit columns in the trial balance is wrong.

2. **Copying of Balances From Ledger Accounts to Trial Balance is Wrong.** A mistake could have been made in copying the balances from the original to the trial balance. Or perhaps one account balance has been listed twice—or omitted completely.

3. **Subtraction Wrong in Determining Individual Account Balances.** When the footing on one side of the account was subtracted from the footing of the other side to find the account balance, perhaps a mistake was made in the subtraction.

4. **Footing of Accounts Incorrect.** The additions of debit and credit sides of an individual account might have been done incorrectly.

5. **Original Entry Was Incorrect.** If the mistake cannot be found in the trial balance or in the addition and subtraction involved in balancing the individual accounts, then it will be necessary to check the original entries in the accounts. The amount entered may be wrong, only half of a transaction may have been entered (just the debit and not the credit, etc.) or a debit item may have been entered as a credit, etc.

6. **Hints for Finding Errors in Trial Balance.** There are several suggestions which may help in finding the error in the trial balance.

a. DIVIDING BY TWO. Divide the difference in the trial balance by two, and look for an entry in this amount. This will help you to find a debit that has been entered as a credit or vice versa.

b. DIVIDING BY NINE. If the difference in the trial balance is evenly divisible by 9, there is a chance a set of figures has been mixed up or transposed. For example, if you had entered $782 as $728, your trial balance would show a difference of $54, which is divisible by 9.

CORRECTING ERRORS

If there is an error in the *ledger, do not erase.* The ledger is a bookkeeping record, and errors in bookkeeping records are corrected by crossing out, not by erasing. Errors in pencil footings or in the trial balance may be corrected by erasing or crossing out, since these are not permanent bookkeeping records.

1. **Errors in the Ledger Accounts.** If a mistake is found in a number in the ledger account, cross out the incorrect entry, and write the correct number above it.

   Sometimes an item has been written on the wrong side of the account (for example, the debit side instead of the credit side). Cross out the item, and write it on the correct side.

   If the item has been written in the wrong ledger account, cross it out and write it in the correct account.

   If the pencil footing or the account balance is wrong because a mistake has been made in addition or subtraction, you may erase it and write the correct number in.

2. **Errors in the Trial Balance.** The trial balance is not a permanent bookkeeping record. Therefore, it may be corrected by erasures as well as by crossing out. If an item has been omitted in drawing up the trial balance, insert it in its proper place.

ALL TRIAL-BALANCE ERRORS DO NOT SHOW UP IN TRIAL BALANCE

It is very important to realize that all ledger errors do not show up in the trial balance. A balanced trial balance just shows that the total of debits entered in the accounts equals the total of credits entered. It is possible, however, *to make other kinds of errors,* and for the trial balance to balance.

1. **Omissions.** Sometimes a transaction is omitted *completely* from the ledger—with *no* debits or credits entered to record it. In such a case, trial balance will be in balance, but ledger accounts are incomplete and inaccurate, since this transaction is not recorded.

2. **Recording Entries in the Wrong Account.** If an entry has been recorded in the *wrong account* (misposted), this may not show up in the trial balance. For example, a purchase of merchandise of $100 for cash can be entered by crediting cash for $100 and then debiting *office furniture,* rather than *merchandise,* for $100. Since the debits and credits are equal, the trial balance will balance. But the wrong account has been debited, and neither the merchandise nor the office furniture account is now accurate.

3. **Offsetting Mistakes.** Sometimes, two similar mistakes will be made which offset each other. For example, a check for $500 may be received from a customer in payment of his bill. A mistake is made and *only $50* is credited to accounts receivable and debited to cash. Since equal debits and credits of $50 have been entered, the trial balance will balance. But the ledger is not right.

4. **Transactions Entered Twice.** A set of debits and credits resulting from one transaction may be entered two times in the ledger accounts. The trial balance will balance since equal credits and debits have been entered, but the ledger accounts are wrong.

TEST YOURSELF

Chapters 6 and 7

True or False:

1. Ledger accounts are kept only for items found on the balance sheet.
2. The chart of accounts lists only asset accounts.
3. To open a ledger account for an asset, list the amount of the asset on the debit side of the account.
4. An increase in a liability is shown by crediting the liability ledger account.
5. Each time an entry is made in a ledger account, *year, date* and *month* must be written in.
6. A trial balance which is in balance shows that there are *no mistakes* in the ledger.
7. When a transaction is recorded in a ledger, this is called footing the account.
8. A trial balance is in balance when the total of debit balances equals the total of credit balances.
9. Errors in the *ledger* should be corrected by *erasing* the wrong entry and writing in the correct one.
10. A double line should be drawn under a trial balance that is in balance to show that it balances.
11. A debit and a credit of *equal amount* have been omitted from the ledger. No other mistakes have been made. The trial balance will balance.

12. A transaction has been recorded *twice* in the ledger, with two sets of equal debits and credits. No other mistakes have been made. The trial balance will balance.
13. To open a ledger account for a liability, debit the liability account.
14. To record an expense in the ledger, credit the expense account.
15. To record income in the ledger, credit the income account.
16. A debit has been recorded in the ledger, but the corresponding credit for the transaction has not been recorded. No other mistakes have been made. The trial balance will *not* balance.
17. Some ledger accounts may have entries on only one side.
18. To record a decrease in cash, debit the cash account.

Identify or Explain.

Trial balance.
Balancing the account.
Footing the account.
Chart of Account.
"Out of balance" trial balance.
Ledger.

The Journal 8

DIRECT LEDGER ACCOUNTING

It might be possible to keep records of business transactions by entering them as they happen directly into the ledger accounts. However, this is *not* the usual procedure. Direct ledger accounting would be difficult for several reasons.

1. **Difficult to Retrace a Transaction.** *Each half* of a business transaction is entered in a separate ledger account, and there is frequently no easy way to tell from one entry just what the business transaction was. For example, a debit of $100 may be found in the cash account. All that this tells us is that the company's cash was increased by $100. There is no way to know if this cash resulted from a sale, a payment of an outstanding bill by a customer, a loan from the bank, etc. The only way to find out would be to check through all the other ledger accounts until a credit for the same amount on the same date was found, and then try to piece the transaction together.

2. **Transactions Are Not Recorded in Order.** Each ledger account lists only those transactions that affect that particular account. The ledger system does not provide a *single running record* of all business transactions on a day-to-day basis in the order in which they occur.

3. **Difficult to Find Errors.** Often the trial balance doesn't balance, and the cause appears to be that a debit and a credit of unequal amounts have been entered for a single transaction. In order to find the mistake, each individual item in each individual ledger account must be cross-checked until the error appears. This is difficult to do, because there is no simple way to know just where the offsetting entry for a particular debit or credit is. The bookkeeper must check each ledger account to find each offsetting entry. This is difficult and time consuming.

ADVANTAGES OF THE JOURNAL

In order to solve these problems, most bookkeeping systems use *journals.* As each transaction occurs, the debits and credits resulting from it are entered *together* in the journal. Then, later on, they are copied into the individual ledger accounts. Since the journal is the *first* place in which a transaction is recorded, it is called the *book of original entry.*

1. **Journal Is Kept in Chronological Order.** Each transaction is recorded in the journal in the order in which it happens.

2. **Both Halves of Transaction Are Listed Together.** The debits and the credits resulting from each transaction are listed, one under the other, together. This is useful in retracing a transaction. It is also helpful when rechecking to find an error.

3. **Errors Are Reduced.** Both halves of each transaction are listed together. Therefore, the bookkeeper is not likely to record *both* entries as debits or as credits, or to omit one half of the transaction from the record.

JOURNALIZING

The process of recording transactions in the journal is called *journalizing.*

DESCRIPTION OF JOURNAL

The journal is usually a bound volume. Its pages are numbered consecutively. Each page has the name "journal" and the page number at the top. The standard 2-column journal provides columns for listing various kinds of information.

1. **Date.**
   a. YEAR. The year is written only once on each page, at the top of the column, unless the year changes.
   b. MONTH. The month is written at the top of the first column on each page. The month is not written again until the month changes.
   c. DAY. Although the year and month are written *only once* on each page, unless there is a change, the day of the transaction is given for EACH transaction, regardless of whether or not another transaction took place on the same day and is entered above.

2. **Name of Account.** The name of the account to be debited will appear on one line in this

column, with the name of the account to be credited on the next line—slightly indented. (In some bookkeeping systems a very brief explanation of the transaction appears on the third line—e.g., to record cash sales, or to record payment of a bill by J. Jones, etc.)

3. **Post. Ref. Column.**   A space for the number of the ledger account to be debited or credited is provided. This is filled in later on, when each half of the transaction is copied into the ledger. (See posting.)

4. **Debit Amount and Credit Amount.**   The amounts of the debits and credits are recorded in columns provided for this purpose.

JOURNALIZING A TRANSACTION

When a transaction occurs, the bookkeeper receives some kind of record of the transaction—a sales slip, a bill, or so forth. Using this *original business paper*, the bookkeeper must analyze the transaction to determine which accounts are to be debited and which are to be credited. Then, the transaction can be journalized.

1. **Fill in Date of Transaction.**   Write day in date column. (Do not rewrite month or year unless they have changed since the preceding entry, or you are starting a new page.)

2. **Record the Transaction.**   In the description column, on the same line with the date, write the *exact name* of the ledger account to be debited, and write the amount in the debit column. On the next line, indented slightly, write the name of the account to be credited. Write the amount to be credited in the credit column.

3. **Post. Ref. Column.**   For the time being, leave this column blank. (Use of this column is explained later in the chapter under "posting.")

EXAMPLE 1:

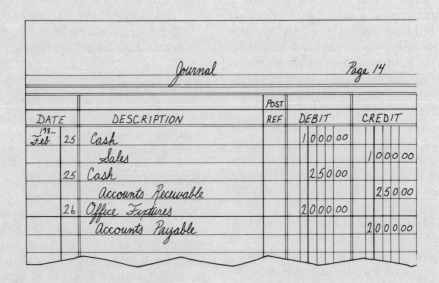

The above Example 1 shows how three transactions were journalized. The first is a cash sale for $1,000.00. Cash is increased, so debit cash account. Sales account is credited.

The second transaction shows receipt of cash from a customer in payment of his account receivable. Cash is increased (debit cash) and accounts receivable is decreased (credit accounts receivable).

The third transaction, on February 26th, shows *purchase* by the company of $2,000.00 worth of office fixtures, which were charged. Office fixtures are increased (debit office fixtures) and accounts

payable, a liability account, is also increased (credit accounts payable).

SIMPLE AND COMPOUND JOURNAL ENTRIES

Many business transactions result in one debit and one credit. For example, a cash sale for $100 results in a $100 debit to cash and a $100 credit to sales. Such a journal entry, with *one debit* and *one credit* is called a simple journal entry. (See March 2nd entry in Example 2.)

Sometimes, however, a transaction will result in *more than one* credit or more than one debit. For example, a $100 sale is made. The customer pays $50 in cash and charges the other $50. Sales account is credited with the entire $100, but there are two offsetting debit entries: $50 is debited to cash, and $50 to accounts receivable. Such a journal entry with several debits and/or credits is called a compound journal entry. (See March 3rd entry in Example 2.)

EXAMPLE 2:

DATE		DESCRIPTION	POST REF	DEBIT	CREDIT
Mar	2	Cash		100 00	
		Sales			100 00
	3	Cash		50 00	
		Accounts Receivable		50 00	
		Sales			100 00

Journal — Page 15

POSTING

At some point after each transaction has been journalized, the debits and credits are copied from the journal into the ledger accounts. This is called posting. Posting should be done often enough so that the ledger accounts are reasonably up to date. Some businesses post daily from journal to ledger, others once a week or even less often, depending on the nature and needs of the business.

1. **Post the Amount.** The first step in posting is to open the ledger account which is to be debited. Copy the amount of the debit from the journal to the debit side of that ledger account.
2. **Copy the Date.** Record the date in the ledger account as explained in Chapter 6.
3. **The Post. Ref. Column.** In the post. ref. column on the debit side of the ledger account where you are working, write the *number of the page* of the journal from which you are copying the transaction. (This will make it easy to check back to the journal in the future if necessary.)
4. **Write Ledger Account Number in Post. Ref. Column of Journal.** Write the number of the ledger account which you are debiting in the post. ref. column of the journal. This serves two purposes.

a. SIMPLIFIES FUTURE CHECKING.
b. SHOWS THAT TRANSACTION HAS BEEN POSTED TO THE LEDGER. Once the ledger account number has been written in the journal, the bookkeeper knows when he looks at the journal that *this particular journal entry has been posted.* He will not post it again into the journal. A blank space in the post. ref. column of the journal means that the item has not as yet been posted in the ledger.
5. **Repeat Same Procedure for Account that Is to Be Credited.**
6. **Alternative Procedure.** Some bookkeepers find it easier to post a group of several debits, and then the offsetting credits, rather than to complete the debit and credit from each transaction before going on to the next. As long as care is taken to write the ledger number in the post. ref. column of the journal when an amount has been posted, mistakes will be avoided and this method is satisfactory too.

The following example shows the method of journalizing a transaction where a cash sale of $50.00 was made.

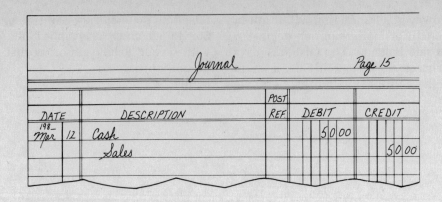

The journal entry is then posted to the cash account (a debit) in the ledger,

Cash								*account #110*
DATE	ITEMS	POST REF.	DEBIT	DATE	ITEMS	POST REF.	CREDIT	
198— Mar 12		15	50 00					

and to the sales account (a credit) in the ledger,

Sales								*account #410*
DATE	ITEMS	POST REF.	DEBIT	DATE	ITEMS	POST REF.	CREDIT	
				198— Mar 12		15	50 00	

and the *post. ref.* column of the journal is filled in with ledger account numbers.

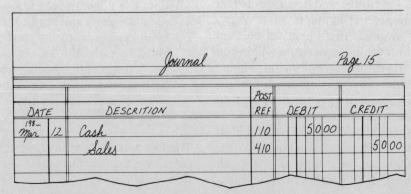

7. **Cross-Referencing.** We have seen that as part of posting:
   a. The journal page number on which the transaction is originally recorded is written in the ledger account in the post. ref. column.
   b. The ledger account number to which debits or credits are posted is written in the post. ref. column of the journal.

This is called *cross-referencing*, and simplifies future checking. The journal page number and the ledger account number are called *post-marks*.

True or False.

1. Ledger is a book of original entry.
2. A separate page in the journal is provided for each ledger account.
3. A journal is usually a bound volume consisting of numbered pages.
4. For each transaction, an equal amount of debits and credits must be journalized.
5. In entering transactions from the journal to the ledger, always post the *amount first.*
6. Recording transactions in the *journal* is called posting.
7. The number of the journal page from which a transaction has been copied is written in the post. ref. column of the ledger account.
8. You can find the account number of the account to which a journal entry has been posted by looking in the post. ref. column of the journal.
9. In posting to a ledger account, you must always rewrite the year and month in the date column for each transaction.
10. Items listed as debits in the journal are posted as debits to the ledger account.

Define or Explain.

1. Journalizing.
2. Book of original entry.
3. Compound journal entry.
4. Posting.
5. Post-marks.

Essay Questions.

1. Give three reasons why most bookkeeping systems find it advantageous to record a transaction in a journal first, rather than directly in ledger accounts.
2. Explain the cross-referencing system which enables a bookkeeper to determine quickly the account to which a journal entry has been posted, and the journal page from which a ledger entry was copied.

Multi-Columnar Journals | 9

MULTI-COLUMNAR JOURNALS

A multi-columnar journal is a journal which provides special columns for recording certain kinds of debits and credits, and also has general debit and general credit columns for recording all debits and credits not entered in the special columns. There are 4-column journals, 6-, 8- or even more column journals, depending on the needs of the business.

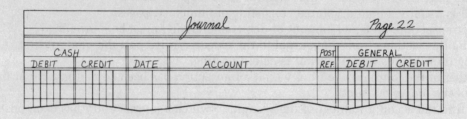

A 4-column journal is illustrated above, with special columns for cash credit and cash debit. General debit and credit columns are also provided.

USE OF MULTI-COLUMNAR JOURNALS

The 4-column Journal: In most businesses, many of the transactions will affect the cash account in one way or another, so many of the entries in the journal will deal with the cash account (i.e., when cash sales take place, or cash is received in payment of customers' accounts receivable, or when the firm pays its own bills, etc.). Each time such a transaction is journalized in the 2-column journal illustrated in the preceding chapter, the name of the account—cash—must be written in. Also, each cash debit or credit must be posted separately into the cash ledger account. A 4-column multi-columnar journal with separate cash debit and cash credit columns is more efficient than the 2-column journal for several reasons.

1. **Time Is Saved in Journalizing.** It is not necessary to write the word "cash" on a separate line each time a transaction affecting the cash account occurs. All that is necessary is to write the amount in the cash debit or credit column.
2. **Time Is Saved in Posting.** When the journal is posted into the ledger, time is also saved.

Each cash item does not have to be posted separately. Instead, only the *totals* of the cash debit and cash credit column are posted. This is much simpler than posting each item individually.

JOURNALIZING IN THE 4-COLUMN JOURNAL

Journalizing in the 4-column journal follows the same principles as journalizing in the 2-column journal. The first step is to analyze the transaction and to decide which accounts are to be debited and which are to be credited.

1. **Transactions Involving Cash Account.** The 4-column journal provides special columns for recording *cash debits* and *cash credits*. When a transaction occurs which involves the cash account, write the name of the other account involved in the description column. If this account is to be debited, write the amount in the *general debit* column. If it is to be credited, write the amount in the *general credit* column.

   Then, *on the same line,* write the amount to be debited or credited to cash in the *cash debit* or *cash credit* account. At no point is the name—cash account—written in.

   Note that only one line is used in this 4-column journal to record a sale or purchase for cash.

24

CASH		DATE	DESCRIPTION	POST REF	GENERAL	
DEBIT	CREDIT				DEBIT	CREDIT
50 00		Mar 20	Sales			50 00
60 00		21	Accounts Receivable			60 00
	10 00	22	Supplies		10 00	

The March 20th transaction entered above records a cash sale of $50.00. The sales account is to be credited with $50.00 and the cash account is to be debited. The date is filled in, and the account name—sales—is written in the description column. Then the general credit column is credited with $50.00. The offsetting debit is shown by writing in $50.00 in the *cash debit column on the same line.*

The March 21st transaction records the receipt of $60.00 in cash in payment of an account receivable.

The March 22nd transaction records payments of $10.00 in cash for supplies. Since cash is decreased, the $10.00 is recorded in the cash credit column. Supplies are increased, and this is shown by entering a debit of $10.00 in the general debit column.

2. Transactions Involving Only-Non-Cash Accounts. Some business transactions will not affect the cash account at all. For example, a sale for credit will affect only the sales account and accounts receivable account. In such a case, the regular journalizing procedures used in the 2-column journal are followed. First, the date and amount to be debited are written in. The amount to be debited is listed in the *general debit column.* Then, on the next line, the name of the account to be credited is written, and the amount to be credited is written in the *general credit column.* Since the cash account is not involved, no entries at all are made in the cash credit or cash debit columns.

Note that transactions involving accounts for which *there are no special columns* require *two* lines for journalizing.

CASH		DATE	DESCRIPTION	POST REF	GENERAL	
DEBIT	CREDIT				DEBIT	CREDIT
		Apr 5	Accounts Receivable		100 00	
			Sales			100 00

The example above records a credit sale for $100.00. Since the cash account was not involved, two lines are required to journalize this transaction. Since the cash account was not involved, no entries are made in the cash debit or credit column.

POSTING FROM THE 4-COLUMN JOURNAL

When posting from a 4-column journal to the individual ledger accounts, the *totals* of the cash debit and cash credit columns are posted at the end of the month to the cash account. *Each individual item* in the general debit and general credit column is posted separately, to its appropriate account, at frequent intervals *during the month.*

  1. Posting Non-Cash Items. Posting of non-cash entries is handled in the ordinary manner de-

scribed in the preceding chapter. It is done at frequent intervals during the month. The amount, date and journal page number are recorded in the appropriate ledger account for each non-cash item. The ledger account number is written in the journal post. ref. column to show that the posting has been done.

  2. Posting Cash Items. The cash ledger account is obtained and the *total* in the *cash debit column* of the journal is entered on the left or debit side of the cash account. The date, and number of the journal page from which the total was taken (post. ref.), are also recorded.

Then the total of the cash credit column of the journal is entered on the credit side of the cash ledger account, with the date and journal page number.

To show that the totals of the cash credit and

debit columns of the journal have been posted, the number of the cash account is written in parentheses below the double line in the journal. (See Figure 15.)

CASH		DATE	DESCRIPTION	POST REF.	GENERAL	
DEBIT	CREDIT				DEBIT	CREDIT
100 00		198— Sept. 1	Sales	410		100 00
	50 00	2	Accounts Payable	211	50 00	
		2	Accounts Receivable	120	10 00	
			Sales	410		10 00
		10	Merchandise	130	200 00	
			Accounts Payable	211		200 00
20 00		25	Accounts Receivable	120		20 00
120 00	50 00				260 00	330 00
(110)	(110)				(✓)	(✓)

Only totals of cash column entries are posted.

Items in these 2 general columns have been posted individually during the month.

Note that only *totals* of cash entries are posted from this journal to the cash ledger account. However, since *each item in the general debit and general credit column of the journal has been posted individually,* there is no need to post the totals of the general debit and general credit columns, *and they are not posted.* Many bookkeepers place a check mark in parentheses below the double line in the general debit and general credit columns just to show that no further posting is required.

3. **Totaling.** Before month-end posting of special column totals from the 4-column journal (or any multi-columnar journal) many bookkeepers suggest totaling all the individual columns, and then seeing if the sum of all the credit columns equals the sum of all the debit columns. This is a check on whether all entries have been made, since, if they have, total debits should, of course, equal total credits. If they are equal, double lines are drawn below all the money columns.

4. **The Journal After Posting.** The totals of the cash credit and cash debit columns were posted directly to the cash account, and the number of that account—110—is written below the total to show that posting has been completed. Each of the items in the general debit and general credit columns were posted individually, and the number of the account to which each was posted appears in the post. ref. column to show that posting has been completed. A check beneath general debit and credit totals shows that no further posting is necessary.

5. **Ledger After Posting — The Cash Account.**

	Cash							Account #110
DATE	ITEM	POST REF	DEBIT	DATE	ITEM	POST REF	CREDIT	
198— Sept. 30		J25	120 00	198— Sept. 30		J25	50 00	

Total of cash debit column in multi-columnar journal.

Total of cash credit column in multi-columnar journal.

The cash account shows how the totals of the cash debit and cash credit columns of the multi-column journal were posted at the month end. J25 in the post. ref. column refers to page 25 of the general journal.

OTHER FORMS OF MULTI-COLUMNAR JOURNALS

The 4-column multi-columnar journal has been illustrated here, but there are many other possible forms of multi-columnar journals. For example, a retail establishment might want to provide columns for recording salary expense, advertising expense, office expense and miscellaneous expense. It might use a 6-column journal with separate columns for these four items, and two additional columns for general debit and general credit. In this way, when time comes to post from the ledger, only the totals of salary expense, advertising expense, office expense and miscellaneous expense need be entered into their ledger accounts, rather than requiring numerous separate entries.

The exact form of a multi-columnar journal will depend on the needs of the business.

	DATE	DESCRIPTION	POST REF	GENERAL DEBIT	GENERAL CREDIT	SALARY EXPENSE DEBIT	ADVERTISING EXPENSE DEBIT	OFFICE EXPENSE DEBIT	MISCELLANEOUS EXPENSE DEBIT
1									
2	June 1	Cash			100 00	100 00			
3	2	Accounts Payable			50 00		50 00		
4	5	Accounts Payable			10 00			10 00	
5	7	Cash			5 00				5 00
6	12	Merchandise		500 00					
7		Accounts Payable			500 00				
8	14	Office Equipment		100 00					
9		Cash			100 00				
10									

Journal — Page 30

Example of 6-Column Multi-Columnar Journal

TEST YOURSELF

Chapter 9

The Williams Company uses a 4-column multi-columnar journal with cash debit and cash credit columns, and general debit and general credit columns.

CASH DEBIT	CASH CREDIT	DATE	ITEM	POST REF.	GENERAL DEBIT	GENERAL CREDIT

Journal — Page 7

1. How many lines would be required to journalize a *cash* sale?
2. How many lines would be required to journalize a *credit* sale?
3. Is each entry in the cash debit column posted *individually* to the cash ledger account? When is the amount recorded in the cash debit column posted to the cash ledger account?
4. Is each entry in the general debit column posted individually to its appropriate ledger account?
5. Are the totals of the cash credit and cash debit column posted? Where are they posted? When are they posted?
6. Are the totals of the general credit and general debit column posted? Why?
7. If the Williams Company used a 5-column journal with a special column for income from investments, when would the total of the income from investment column be posted?

The Accounts Receivable Ledger | 10

TRADING ON CREDIT

In most businesses, trading on credit exists. This is an arrangement in which goods are exchanged with the understanding that at the end of a given period of time, the customer will pay for them. Charge accounts are an example of individual *trading on credit*.

ACCOUNTS RECEIVABLE

Debts owed by its customers to a firm resulting from trading on credit are called *accounts receivable*. These debts owed to the firm are listed as accounts receivable under the assets of the firm on its balance sheet. There is also a general ledger account called accounts receivable, which lists the total amounts owed in all customer accounts with the firm.

ACCOUNTS RECEIVABLE LEDGER

Most businesses, however, do not find it satisfactory to list all customer debts *together* in *one* general ledger accounts receivable account. Businesses usually keep a separate record of each individual customer's account, rather than lumping all customer indebtedness together. This is done by having a subsidiary account receivable ledger (or *customer's ledger*).

1. **Description of Accounts Receivable Ledger.** An accounts receivable (or customer's) ledger is a ledger consisting of a separate page or sheet for each customer on which his credit purchases and payments are recorded. The individual pages are kept in alphabetical order, according to the names of the customers. Each sheet is headed with customer's name and address. By consulting a particular customer's sheet in this accounts receivable ledger, the bookkeeper can find out at any time the exact indebtedness of the customer.

2. **Posting to the Accounts Receivable Ledger.** All credit sales and payments of outstanding bills by customers are posted to the individual customer account in the accounts receivable ledger, and *not* to the accounts receivable account in the general ledger. Each ledger page in the accounts receivable ledger has three money columns—debit, credit and debit balance.

a. SALES ON ACCOUNT. When a customer buys merchandise (or services) on account, his account receivable is increased and should be *debited* when the transaction is journalized. When the journal entry is to be posted, the customer's account in the accounts receivable ledger is opened, and the amount is posted in the debit column. The date of the transaction is entered in the date column, and the journal page from which the transaction is posted is recorded in the post. ref. column. Finally, the debit balance is computed by adding the new purchase to any balance previously outstanding.

DATE	ITEM	POST REF.	DEBIT	CREDIT	DEBIT BALANCE
19— Sept 13		10	200 00		200 00
21		14		50 00	250 00

Holiday Farms Co.
151 North Street, White Plains

The accompanying ledger sheet for Holiday Farms Company, a customer of Green Corporation, is part of Green Corporation's accounts receivable ledger, in which each credit customer has a similar sheet. Two purchases on credit are recorded. On September 13th, Holiday bought $200 worth of merchandise, and on September 21st, Holiday bought $50 worth of merchandise. The total debit balance (or amount Holiday owed), was $250 on September 21st.

b. PAYMENTS OF ACCOUNTS BY CUSTOMERS. When a customer pays his bills, his account is reduced. The journal shows a credit to his account receivable. This credit journal entry is then posted to the customer's ledger sheet in the accounts receivable ledger. The fol-

lowing entry shows how a payment of $100 was recorded in Holiday Farms Company ledger sheet. First the amount is posted to the credit column, then the date, post. ref. page of the journal and the new debit balance are recorded. Note the new debit balance, which has been reduced by the payment of $100 from $250 to $150.

	Holiday Farms Co. 151 North Street, White Plains				
DATE	ITEM	POST REF.	DEBIT	CREDIT	DEBIT BALANCE
195— Sept 13		10	200 00		200 00
21		14	50 00		250 00
25		16		100 00	150 00

3. Usefulness of Accounts Receivable Ledger.

The student should observe that it is much easier for a firm to keep track of its accounts receivable through use of a subsidiary accounts receivable ledger than if all accounts were listed in one general ledger account.

a. BILLING AND CREDIT PROCEDURES SIMPLIFIED. Each customer's total indebtedness is listed in one place and can be obtained quickly for billing purposes or to check whether or not to extend more credit. If only one all-inclusive general ledger accounts receivable account were used, the bookkeeper would have to check all the entries in the account and then extract only those dealing with the one particular customer.

b. OTHER ACCOUNTING PROCEDURES SIMPLIFIED. If all accounts receivable were entered in only one ledger account consisting of one sheet in the general ledger, then only one bookkeeper could make entries in the accounts at one time. The use of the subsidiary accounts receivable ledger, with individual accounts for each customer, makes it possible for several bookkeepers to work on accounts receivable at one time.

THE CONTROLLING GENERAL LEDGER ACCOUNT

There are times, however, when a businessman wants to know the total of all accounts receivable that he has on his books—for example, when he's preparing a balance sheet. Therefore, when a company uses the separate accounts receivable ledger

to list its individual customer accounts, it also keeps a single summarizing account in the general ledger, in which the sum of all the individual customer accounts receivable balances can be found. This general ledger account, in which the total balances of all the individual accounts receivable are summarized, is called the general ledger accounts receivable controlling account. It is often referred to as the controlling account for the specialized accounts receivable ledger.

1. **Posting to the Accounts Receivable Controlling Account in the General Ledger.** We have seen that each individual credit sale or bill payment by a customer is posted to the individual customer's account in the subsidiary accounts receivable ledger. This is usually done on a daily basis, in order to keep accounts up to date. At the end of the month, one dollar amount—the total of all accounts receivable sales during the month—is posted (as a debit) to the accounts receivable controlling account in the general ledger. Also, at the end of the month, the total amount of payments of accounts receivable made by customers during the month, is posted (as a credit) to the controlling account. (See chapters on sales journal and cash payments journal for details on month-end posting to the accounts receivable controlling account. These chapters explain how the month-end total of debits and credits are obtained.)

In other words, the controlling accounts receivable account in the general ledger is posted with the two month-end items—a dollar total of all *increases* in accounts receivable resulting from purchases on account by customers during the month (*a debit*), and a total of all the decreases in accounts receivable occurring during the month because of payments received (a credit). *It is a summary account or controlling account for all the specific information about transactions which have been posted to the individual customer accounts in the accounts receivable ledger.*

General Ledger Controlling Account for Accounts Receivable

The above is an example of an accounts receivable general ledger controlling account. Month-end entries have been made in the account. A debit of $740.00 was entered, showing that individual customers increased their accounts receivable by $740.00 during the month. A credit of $540.00 was entered, representing total payments or reductions of accounts receivable by customers occurring during the month. (The post. ref. entries S-12 and CR-5 refer to sales journal and cash receipts journal. See chapters on these journals for more details.)

2. **Importance of the Controlling Account.** The controlling account in the general ledger is very important as a source of summarized information about the total amount of accounts receivable. It also simplifies preparation of month-end worksheets, trial balances and balance sheets, since only one account need be handled rather than all the individual customer accounts in the accounts receivable ledger.

SUMMARY

In most businesses, increases and decreases in accounts receivable occurring during the month are posted to the individual customer accounts in a subsidiary accounts receivable ledger, rather than to a single general ledger accounts receivable account.

At the end of the month, summarizing entries are made in the general ledger accounts receivable controlling account. This controlling account is debited with the total of all the increases in accounts receivable occurring in individual customer accounts during the month, and is credited with one amount representing all reductions in accounts receivable due to payments, etc., from all the individual customers.

TEST YOURSELF

Chapter 10

True or False.

1. Each customer who buys on credit has a separate account in the accounts receivable ledger.
2. When a customer buys merchandise on credit, accounts receivable are increased, so the accounts receivable account is *credited.*
3. Each individual account in the accounts receivable ledger is included in the general ledger.
4. When a customer *pays* his account, accounts receivable are *credited.*
5. A purchase by a customer on account will increase the debit balance on the customer's account.
6. The accounts receivable ledger is a separate ledger with a controlling account (the accounts receivable controlling account) in the general ledger.
7. The total of all amounts debited to the individual customers' accounts during the month is debited at the month end to the accounts receivable controlling account.
8. Each time a customer buys goods for credit, the transaction is posted from the journal to the accounts receivable controlling account in the general ledger.

9. Each time a customer pays off part of his account, the transaction is posted directly from the journal to the accounts receivable controlling account in the general ledger.
10. Purchases on account and payments on account by customers are posted from the journal to the individual customer accounts in the accounts receivable ledger.
11. At the month end, the balance in the accounts receivable controlling account should equal the sum of the balances in all the individual accounts in the accounts receivable ledger.
12. The page number of the journal page from which the transaction has been posted is written in the post. ref. column of the customer's ledger.
13. Purchases on account by customers are debited to customers' accounts.
14. Payments on account by customers are debited to customers' accounts.

The Accounts Payable Ledger | 11

In business, some of the purchases that are made will be paid for in cash at the time of purchase (example: stamps that are bought at the post office). But most purchases are made with the understanding that they will be paid for at a stated later date. This is called purchasing on account, and the monies which the purchaser owes in connection with such a purchase are called accounts payable.

ACCOUNTS PAYABLE

Debts which a business incurs arising out of *the ordinary use of credit in its everyday purchase of goods or services* are called accounts payable. (Debts arising out of more formal borrowing arrangements, such as borrowing from banks are *not* included as accounts payable. They are called notes payable.) The total amount of accounts payable is listed under this name on the balance sheet, and in the general ledger.

ACCOUNTS PAYABLE LEDGER

Many businesses, however, do not find it useful to record all their unpaid bills directly in the one accounts payable general ledger account. They prefer to keep a separate listing of transactions with each creditor. This is done by keeping a separate accounts payable ledger.

1. **Description of Accounts Payable Ledger.** An accounts payable ledger (also called *creditors' ledger*) is a subsidiary ledger. It is usually a loose-leaf binder or a set of cards, organized alphabetically. A separate sheet or card is provided for each creditor to whom the firm owes money. Each sheet or card is headed with the name and the address of the creditor. Spaces are provided for listing date, debits, credits and credit balance. There is also a post. ref. column.

The above is an example of an individual card or sheet in Jones Company's accounts payable ledger. Harris Supply Company is one of the firms from whom Jones buys merchandise on account. Every time a purchase is made from Harris or a payment made to Harris, Jones will record this on Harris' ledger sheet.

2. **Advantages of Accounts Payable Ledger.** There are several advantages to using a separate accounts payable ledger, rather than entering all credit purchases directly in a single general ledger accounts payable account.
   a. CENTRALIZATION OF INFORMATION. An accounts payable ledger provides a separate

sheet for each creditor. By consulting this one sheet, a bookkeeper can have all the information about purchases, payments and amount due a particular supplier, in one place. Otherwise, it would be necessary to extract all this information from the general ledger accounts payable account, where it would be entered along with all the other accounts payable transactions.

b. SEVERAL BOOKKEEPERS CAN WORK ON BOOKS AT ONE TIME. If there is only one general ledger accounts payable account, then only one bookkeeper can work on it at a time. When an entire accounts payable ledger is used to record credit purchases and payments, then several bookkeepers can record accounts payable transactions, with each working on several sheets from the accounts payable ledger.

3. **Posting to the Accounts Payable Ledger.** Each time the firm obtains something on account, the amount of money it owes (its liabilities) are increased. As we know, an increase in a liability account is recorded by a credit to the account. Therefore, each time a purchase on account is made, the journal entry will include a credit to accounts payable. When a firm uses an accounts payable ledger, this credit is posted from the journal into the *individual creditor's account*

in the accounts payable ledger, *not into the general ledger accounts payable account.*

Similarly, a payment by the firm of an outstanding accounts payable will result in a journal entry of a debit to accounts payable. This will be posted as a debit to the individual account in the accounts payable ledger.

a. PURCHASES ON ACCOUNT. An example of a ledger account card from the Jones Company accounts payable ledger for Harris Supply Company is given. On Jan. 10th, Jones bought $512 of merchandise from Harris on account, resulting in an account payable owed to Harris. The journal entry would show an increase in merchandise (debit) and an increase in accounts payable (credit). In posting the transaction from the journal to Harris' sheet in the accounts payable ledger, first the amount is posted to the credit column, then the date and post. ref. columns are completed. The journal page number from which the transaction is posted is written in the post. ref. column. The new credit balance is written in the last column. This is the total amount of money now owed by the Jones Company to Harris Supply, and includes the previous outstanding bill of $100 resulting from an earlier purchase.

DATE		ITEM	POST REF.	DEBIT	CREDIT	CREDIT BALANCE
Jan.	4		P4		100 00	100 00
	10		P6		512 00	612 00

Posting a Credit Purchase to Accounts Payable Ledger

b. PAYMENTS. When a company pays an outstanding bill, its accounts payable is debited. This debit is posted from the journal to the individual creditor's account in the accounts payable ledger. The following example shows how a payment by the Jones Company of its debt to Harris would be posted from the journal into Harris' sheet in the accounts payable ledger. First, the amount

of the payment is written in the debit column, then date and post. ref. columns are completed. Finally, a blank line is placed in the credit balance column to show that there is now no balance due Harris. (If Jones had not paid its entire bill, then the credit balance column would show the amount still outstanding.)

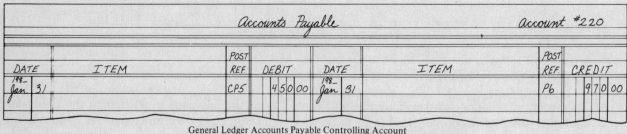

DATE	ITEM	POST REF.	DEBIT	CREDIT	CREDIT BALANCE
198— Jan 4		P4		100 00	100 00
10		P6		512 00	512 00
31		CP7	612 00		

Posting a Payment to Accounts Payable Ledger

ACCOUNTS PAYABLE CONTROLLING ACCOUNT

When a separate accounts payable ledger is kept, an accounts payable controlling account is maintained in the general ledger.

1. **Use of Controlling Account.** At the end of the month, this account is debited with a single figure representing all the individual debits that have been entered in the individual accounts in the accounts payable ledger during the month. It is credited with a single figure, representing all credits entered in the individual accounts payable during the month. (This information is obtained in a summarized form from the purchase journal and from the cash payments journal—see Chapters 14 and 16.)

2. **Relationship Between Accounts Payable Ledger and the Controlling Account.** The accounts payable controlling account in the general ledger serves as a single controlling account in which one can find a summary of all the individual transactions that have been posted to the individual creditor accounts in the accounts payable ledger. At the end of the month, after the totals have been posted to the controlling account, the balance in the controlling account will equal the sum of the balances in all the individual accounts in the accounts payable ledger.

3. **Example of Accounts Payable Controlling Account in the General Ledger.** The following example shows how month-end entries would be made in the accounts payable controlling account in the general ledger. The debit figure represents all reductions in accounts payable occurring during the month, and is posted from the cash payments journal (see Chapter 16). The credit figure represents all increases in accounts payable, and is posted from the purchase journal (see Chapter 14). Both these figures represent the totals of all the individual debits and credits that have been posted to the individual accounts in the accounts payable ledger during the month. After the controlling account was ruled and balanced, the balance in the account would be the total amount of accounts payable owed by the firm to its creditors.

				Accounts Payable			Account #220					
DATE	ITEM	POST REF.	DEBIT	DATE	ITEM	POST REF.	CREDIT
198— Jan 31		CP5	450 00	198— Jan 31		P6	970 00

General Ledger Accounts Payable Controlling Account

SUMMARY

In most businesses, debits and credits to accounts payable are posted on a daily (or other frequent) basis to the individual creditor's accounts in a subsidiary accounts payable ledger.

At the end of the month, a summary of entries is made in the general ledger accounts payable controlling account. The account is debited with the total of all individual debits entered in individual accounts in the accounts payable ledger. The total is obtained from the cash payments journal. The account is credited with the total of all individual credits posted into the individual accounts in the accounts payable ledger. This total is obtained from the purchase journal.

At the end of the month, the balance in the controlling account equals the sum of the balances in the accounts in the subsidiary accounts payable ledger.

TEST YOURSELF

Chapter 11

Multiple Choice.

1. Harry Jones buys merchandise on account from the Green Manufacturing Company. The liability owed by Harry Jones arising out of the purchase is called _____.

    (a) accounts payable (b) accounts receivable (c) notes payable

2. Another name for the accounts payable ledger is _____.

    (a) accounts payable controlling account (b) creditors' ledger
    (c) customers' ledger (d) purchases journal

3. An accounts payable ledger is _____.

    (a) a book or original entry (b) a controlling account (c) a general ledger account
    (d) a separate ledger in which creditors' accounts are kept

4. In Harry Jones' accounts payable ledger, there is a sheet for Green Company. Every time Harry Jones buys merchandise on account from Green Company, _____.

    (a) Green's account will be debited (b) Green's account will be credited
    (c) the transaction is journalized directly into the controlling account

5. When a firm pays its bills to a creditor, _____.

    (a) the creditor's account in the accounts payable ledger is credited
    (b) the creditor's account in the accounts payable ledger is debited
    (c) the transaction is posted directly from the journal to the general ledger
    (d) the accounts receivable ledger is posted

6. When Harry Jones buys merchandise on credit from Green Company, Green Company's account in the accounts payable ledger_____.

    (a) shows an increased *debit* balance (b) shows an increased *credit* balance
    (c) is not affected

7. To find out how much money Harry Jones owes the Green Company at any given time, _____.

    (a) look in the accounts payable controlling account in Harry Jones' general ledger
    (b) look at the credit balance in Green Company's account in Jones' accounts payable ledger
    (c) look at the last entry in the Jones' journal that concerned Green Company

8. When Harry Jones' bookkeeper enters a *debit* to Green Company's account in Jones' *accounts payable* ledger, it probably means that _____.

    (a) Harry Jones just bought additional goods or services on account from Green Company
    (b) Harry Jones has paid part of the bill he owed to Green Company
    (c) Green Company has bought goods on account from Harry Jones

9. The controlling account for the accounts payable ledger_____.

    (a) shows each individual purchase and payment on account

    (b) is posted daily from the journals

    (c) shows only month-end totals of amounts debited and credited to individual accounts payable accounts during the month

10. The quickest way to find out the total amount of money Harry Jones owes to his creditors at the end of the month would be_____.

    (a) to consult his accounts payable ledger (b) to check the journal entries

    (c) to consult the accounts payable controlling account in the Jones' general ledger

Proving the Accounts Payable and Accounts Receivable Ledgers | 12

PROVING THE ACCOUNTS PAYABLE LEDGER

One way of checking to see if posting from the journals to the individual accounts in the accounts payable ledger has been done accurately is to compare the total of all the individual balances in the ledger with the balance in the controlling account in the general ledger. This is called "proving" (or testing) the accounts payable ledger. It is usually done after the trial balance has been taken. The schedule of accounts payable which is drawn up in connection with proving the accounts payable ledger (see below) is frequently presented along with the trial balance as another sign of the accuracy of the books of the firm.

1. **Theory Behind Proving of Accounts Payable Ledger.** We have observed in earlier chapters that accounts payable items are entered individually in the accounts payable subsidiary ledger from the purchases and cash payments journals (or from the appropriate column in the multi-columnar journal). We have also observed that the total of all accounts payable items was entered at the end of the month (from the column totals) directly into the accounts payable controlling account in the general ledger. Therefore, if all entries have been made correctly, the balance in the controlling account should equal the sum of the balances in all the individual accounts in the accounts payable ledger.

2. **Method of Proving the Accounts Payable Ledger.** A *schedule* or *abstract* is made up, consisting of a listing of all the balances in all the creditor accounts in the accounts payable ledger. They are listed alphabetically by the creditor's name. This is called the *Schedule of Accounts Payable*. This list is totaled, and the total is compared with the balance in the accounts payable controlling account. (This balance was obtained earlier by footing and balancing the controlling account in connection with preparation of the trial balance—see Chapter 6.) If the two totals are the same, the accounts payable ledger has been proven.

Below is an example of a Schedule of Accounts Payable and of the controlling accounts payable account in the general ledger with which it was compared.

HOCHMAN MANUFACTURING CO.
Schedule of Accounts Payable
December 31, 198—

Adams Express	$ 500.00
Becker Laundry	300.00
Crown Groceries, Inc.	100.00
Value Liquor Store	50.00
Total Accounts Payable	$ 950.00

Accounts Payable   *Account #212*

DATE	ITEM	POST REF.	DEBIT	DATE	ITEM	POST REF.	CREDIT
198— Dec 31		CP7	750 00	198— Dec 31		P4	1700 00
31	Balance	✓	950 00				
			1700 00				1700 00
				198— Jan 1	Balance	✓	950 00

PROVING THE ACCOUNTS RECEIVABLE LEDGER

The accuracy of the accounts receivable subsidiary ledger is proven in a manner similar to that used to check the accounts payable ledger.

1. **Theory Behind Proving the Accounts Receivable Ledger.** When the bookkeeper posted from the cash payments and sales journal (or from the multi-columnar journal), she posted items individually to the individual accounts in the accounts receivable ledger. She also posted month-end totals of these items to the controlling accounts receivable account in the general ledger. Therefore, if all entries were made correctly, the sum of the balances of the individual accounts in the subsidiary ledger will equal the balance of the controlling account.

2. **Method of Proving the Accounts Receivable Ledger.** A schedule of accounts receivable is drawn up, consisting of an alphabetical listing of the balance in each individual customer's account in the accounts receivable ledger. This is totaled. The total is compared with the balance in the accounts receivable controlling ac-

count in the general ledger, which has previously been footed and balanced. If the two figures—the total of the accounts receivable and the balance in the controlling account—are equal, the accounts receivable ledger has been proven.

Frequently, the Schedule of Accounts Receivable is presented along with the trial balance as one more indication of the accuracy of the firm's books.

Below is an example of a Schedule of Accounts Receivable. Also shown is the general ledger controlling account—Accounts Receivable.

HOCHMAN MANUFACTURING CO.
Schedule of Accounts Receivable
December 31, 198–

Dover Sole Corp.	$ 300.00
Salada Shrimp Co.	200.00
Tuna Tom Inc.	500.00
Ultra Corp.	100.00
Xtra Good, Inc.	50.00
Wotan Company	100.00
Total Accounts Receivable	$1,250.00

Accounts Receivable   *Account #120*

DATE	ITEM	POST REF.	DEBIT	DATE	ITEM	POST REF.	CREDIT
198– Dec. 31		S6	3000 00	198– Dec. 31		CR5	1750 00
				31	Balance	✓	1250 00
			3000 00				3000 00
Dec. 31	Balance	✓	1250 00				

Specialized Journals: The Sales Journal | 13

SPECIAL JOURNALS

Many small firms use only a general journal in which they record *all* their transactions. Larger firms, however, often find it more efficient to use a system of special journals, *in addition to the general journal.* The most widely used of the special journals are the sales journal, cash payments journal, cash receipts journal and purchase journal.

1. **Use of the Special Journal.** In a system that combines special journals with a general journal, groups of similar transactions are recorded in each special journal. For example, all credit sales would be journalized in the sales journal.
2. **Use of the General Journal.** Those transactions that are not a purchase or sale on account or a purchase or sale for cash are journalized in the general journal.
3. **General Journal and Specialized Journals Are Books of Original Entry.** When a journal system involving specialized journals and a general journal is used, the general journal and the special journal are the books of original entry.

ADVANTAGES OF SPECIAL JOURNALS

The use of a system of special journals along with the general journal provides greater efficiency and accuracy. It also reduces the number of individual entries which must be made in the journal, and the number of entries which must be posted to the ledger.

1. **More Than One Bookkeeper Can Work on the Journal at One Time.** If there were only one book of original entry—one journal—it would be possible for only one bookkeeper to make entries at one time. This would not be practical for large enterprises where so many transactions must be recorded in the journal. When specialized journals are used for different categories of transactions, several bookkeepers can work at one time—each one working on one journal. This also leads to fewer errors, since each bookkeeper can become an expert on the kind of entries made in the particular kind of journal he or she is keeping.
2. **Increased Efficiency Through Grouping of Similar Transactions.** When a specialized journal is used for journalizing, many times only one line is required for each entry (see example below), instead of the two lines frequently needed in a general journal. When posting is done from each special journal to the ledger, in many cases only the total resulting from many transactions need be posted, rather than each individual transaction. Thus, both journalizing and posting are simplified through use of special journals.

THE SALES JOURNAL

One of the most widely used special journals is the sales journal. It is also called the *sales book* or the *sales register.* When a sales journal is used, all sales made on account (all credit sales) are recorded in the sales journal and not in the general journal. It is important to remember that *only sales on account, not cash sales,* are recorded in the sales journal.

1. **Sales Slip.** When a sale is made on account in most businesses, a *sales slip* or *invoice* is filled out by the salesperson or sales or billing department. Each sales slip is numbered. A carbon copy of the sales slip is sent to the bookkeeper as a record of the transaction, and serves as the source of information for journalizing the transaction in the sales journal.

   Sales slips vary with the needs of the business, but usually include most of the following information: sales slip number; name and address of customer; date; description of sale—item, number of units, price per unit, total amount of the sale; freight charges; method of shipment; amount of cash, if any, received, and the amount still due; terms of sale; and name or initials of sales clerk.
2. **Journalizing in the Sales Journal.** When the bookkeeper receives the carbon of the sales slip, she uses this information to record the sale in the journal. The sales journal provides columns for recording the date of the sale, the sales slip or invoice number, name of the customer and the amount still due. (There is also a post. ref. column for use when the sales journal is posted to the ledger.)

		Sales Journal		Page 12	
DATE	INVOICE NO.	ACCOUNT	POST REF.	AMOUNT	
198— Jan 14	115	*Gloria Ernest*		10	00

Each transaction is journalized on one line of the sales journal. The above entry in the sales journal is a record of a sale on account to Gloria Ernest for $10.00, which took place on January 14th. The sales slip number (invoice #) for the transaction was number 115.

3. **Posting From the Sales Journal to the Ledgers.** Posting from the sales journal involves three procedures.

   a. DAILY POSTING OF INDIVIDUAL DEBITS TO INDIVIDUAL CUSTOMER ACCOUNTS IN ACCOUNTS RECEIVABLE SUBSIDIARY LEDGER.

   b. MONTHLY POSTING OF TOTAL TO THE ACCOUNTS RECEIVABLE CONTROLLING ACCOUNT IN GENERAL LEDGER—A DEBIT.

   c. MONTHLY POSTING OF TOTAL TO SALES ACCOUNT IN GENERAL LEDGER—A CREDIT.

4. **Posting to Each Customer's Individual Account.** We saw in Chapter 10 how most firms keep track of their accounts receivable by maintaining a separate account for each customer in a *subsidiary accounts receivable ledger.*

   a. IMPORTANCE OF FREQUENT POSTING TO INDIVIDUAL CUSTOMER ACCOUNTS. It is important for the bookkeeper to keep each customer's account up to date, so that the customer or the credit department can obtain at all times a correct statement of the amount of money the customer owes the firm. In order to do this, frequent posting of the sales journal to the individual customer accounts is essential. In many firms, this is done daily.

   b. METHOD OF POSTING TO INDIVIDUAL CUSTOMER ACCOUNTS. Working from the page in the sales journal, the bookkeeper enters each transaction into the appropriate customer's account. Each customer's account is *debited* for the amount of the transaction.

   (1) AMOUNT. First, the amount is written in the debit side of each customer's ledger account.

   (2) DATE. The date of the transaction is recorded in the ledger.

   (3) POST. REF. The page number of the sales journal page from which the transaction is copied, is written in the post. ref. ledger column. The abbreviation "S" is placed before the page number to show that the entry was originally journalized on a page in the *sales* journal, not the general journal.

   (4) DEBIT BALANCE. The debit balance column in the customer's account is filled in by adding the new amount to the previous balance.

   (5) POST. REF. COLUMN OF JOURNAL. The last step in posting from the sales journal to the individual customer accounts is to put a *checkmark* in the post. ref. column of the sales journal. This shows that the amount has been posted *to the accounts receivable ledger.*

Gloria Ernest
12 Avon Avenue, New York City

DATE		ITEMS	POST REF.	DEBIT		CREDIT		DEBIT BALANCE	
198— Jan	1	*Balance*						50	00
	14		S12	10	00			60	00

40

In this example of a customer's account from the accounts receivable subsidiary ledger, we see how the previous sales journal entry of a sale on account for $10.00 to Gloria Ernest has been posted. The date (Jan 14th), sales journal page number (S12), and amount ($10.00) have been posted, and the new balance, $60.00, entered in the debit balance column. The last step, not shown here, would be to put a checkmark in the post. ref. column of the sales journal where this transaction was journalized, to show that it has been posted to the Gloria Ernest account.

5. **Totaling the Sales Journal at the End of the Month.** At the end of the month, the sales journal is totaled. This is done by adding up all the numbers in the amount column, and writing the total beneath the last entry. A double line is then drawn under the total.

The following example shows how the sales journal has been totaled and ruled at the month's end. The numbers in parentheses under the total (120) (410) are the account numbers of the accounts receivable controlling account and the sales account. After the total is posted to these accounts (see below), the number of the account is written in this manner to show that the final posting has been done.

		Sales Journal		Page 12	
DATE	INVOICE NO.	ACCOUNT	POST REF.	AMOUNT	
199— Jan. 14	115	Gloria Ernest	✓	10	00
18	116	H. J. Corp	✓	40	00
25	117	Roger Green	✓	20	00
31	118	Benj. Harris	✓	25	00
				95	00
				(120) (410)	

6. **Posting Total to the General Ledger Accounts Receivable Controlling Account.** After the sales journal has been totaled at the end of the month, this amount is posted to the accounts receivable controlling account in the general ledger. The amount is written in the debit side of the accounts receivable controlling account, with the date. The page number of the sales journal page is written in the post. ref. column of the ledger account. The final step is to write the number of the accounts receivable controlling account in the *sales journal* in parentheses. It is written below the double line in the total column of the sales journal. This shows that the sales journal total of $95.00 has been posted to the accounts receivable controlling account in the general ledger.

					Accounts Receivable			Account #120		
DATE	ITEM		POST REF.	DEBIT	DATE	ITEM		POST REF.	CREDIT	
199— Jan. 31			S12	95 00						

7. Posting to the General Ledger Sales Account.

The total figure from the sales journal is then posted to the *credit side* of the general ledger sales account. The amount, date and page number of the sales journal are filled in (S–12 in above example). Finally, the number of the sales account is written in parentheses under the total column of the sales journal (next to the number of the accounts receivable controlling account) to show that this total has been posted to the general ledger sales account.

DATE	ITEM	POST REF	DEBIT	DATE	ITEM	POST REF	CREDIT
				198– Jan 31		S12	95 00

Sales   Account #410

SUMMARY

The following points should be remembered in connection with the use of a sales journal:

1. All sales made on *account* are journalized in the sales journal—not the general ledger.
2. Daily postings are made from the sales journal to individual customer accounts. Each account is debited. A checkmark is placed in the post. ref. column of the sales journal to show that the *individual account* has been posted.
3. At the month's end, the sales journal is totaled and ruled. This total is *debited* to the general ledger accounts receivable controlling account. It is *credited* to the general ledger sales account. The *numbers* of these accounts are written below the ruled sales journal total column to show that the postings have been made.

TEST YOURSELF

Chapter 13

True or False.

1. Another name for a sales slip is an invoice.
2. Only *cash* sales are journalized in the sales journal.
3. The sales journal is posted to the accounts *payable* ledger.
4. Daily posting is done from the sales journal to individual accounts in the accounts receivable ledger.
5. The abbreviation S in front of a number in the post. ref. column of an account means that the item was posted from the *general* journal.
6. When the sales journal is posted to customer accounts in the accounts receivable ledger, each customer's account is *debited*.
7. Each entry in the sales journal refers to a transaction in which a customer bought merchandise for credit. Therefore the customer's accounts receivable has been increased.
8. The *number* of the accounts receivable *controlling* account is written in the post. ref. column of the sales journal after each entry is debited to the *individual customer account*.
9. A checkmark is placed in the post. ref. column of the sales journal after each entry is debited to the individual customer account.
10. The month-end total in the sales journal is posted as a *debit* to the sales account.
11. The month-end total in the sales journal is posted as a *debit* to the accounts receivable controlling account.

Specialized Journals: The Purchases Journal | 14

In most businesses, merchandise which the firm buys for resale to its customers is bought on account, not for cash. The bills which the firm owes arising out of these purchases are called *accounts payable*. Some small businesses record all such purchases on account in the *general journal*. This expense (purchases) is journalized as a debit to the purchase account, and the increase in accounts payable is journalized as a credit to the accounts payable account.

PURCHASE JOURNAL

Many businesses, however, use a specialized journal, rather than the general journal, in which to record all purchases made on account. It is a book of original entry and is called a *purchases journal* of a *purchases book* or a *purchase register*.

1. **Use of Invoice.** In many companies, when a buyer wishes to order merchandise, he fills out a *purchase order* and sends it to the supplier from whom he orders the merchandise. He keeps a copy of the purchase order. When the supplier fills the order and ships it to the company, an *invoice* is sent with the merchandise. This purchase invoice received by the buyer serves as the source of information for journalizing the transaction.

   a. DESCRIPTION OF INVOICE. The form of a particular invoice will vary from one company to another, but invoices usually include the following: name and address of company that is selling the merchandise, name and address of buyer, date, invoice number of seller, terms of sale (when payment is due, and discounts if any), freight charges, description of merchandise (including quantity, price per unit, etc.), total amount of bill, and method of shipment.

   b. CHECKING THE INVOICE. When the invoice is received, it is stamped with the date of receipt. It is then checked in three ways.

   (1) AGAINST PURCHASE ORDER. Does the merchandise listed on the invoice agree with what the buyer ordered on his copy of the purchase order?

   (2) AGAINST MERCHANDISE. Does the merchandise listed on the invoice agree with the actual merchandise received? A check is placed next to each amount number on the invoice (i.e., seven dresses) as each amount is checked against the merchandise to show that the stated amount of merchandise was actually received.

   (3) FOR ARITHMETIC ACCURACY. Is the multiplication and addition on the invoice correct? (This is called *verifying the extensions*.) A check is placed next to each dollar amount on the invoice to show that it has been verified.

2. **Journalizing in the Purchases Journal.** The bookkeeper receives the *checked* invoice, and uses it to record the transaction in the purchase journal.

   a. DESCRIPTION OF PURCHASES JOURNAL. The purchases journal consists of numbered pages with columns for recording date invoice was received, from whom the purchase was made, post. ref., and amount of purchase. The illustration below shows how a purchase by the Jones Company of $512 worth of merchandise from Harris Supply Company on January 10th would be journalized in the Jones Company's purchases journal. Note that each transaction is journalized on one line of the purchases journal. The following steps may be followed in journalizing a purchase on account.

   (1) Enter date in date column.

   (2) Write name of seller in account column.

   (3) Enter amount of purchase in amount column.

		Purchases Journal		*Page 6*	
DATE		FROM WHOM PURCHASED	POST REF.	AMOUNT	
198— Jan	10	*Harris Supply*		5 1 2 00	

3. Posting to the Ledger From the Purchases Journal.

Posting the purchases journal to the ledger involves several steps.

a. POSTING TO EACH CREDITOR'S INDIVIDUAL ACCOUNT. We saw in Chapter 12 how most firms find it useful to keep track of amounts owed to each creditor through the use of a subsidiary accounts payable ledger. Therefore, each entry in the purchases journal is posted directly to the individual creditor's account in the accounts payable ledger. This is usually done daily. Each purchase represents an increase in accounts payable, so it is *credited* to the individual account.

Daily posting from the purchases journal to the accounts in the accounts payable ledger may follow this form:

(1) AMOUNT. Amount is written in the credit column.

(2) DATE. Date of receipt of the invoice is written in date column.

(3) CREDIT BALANCE. The new credit balance is determined and entered.

(4) POST. REF. The page number of the purchases journal page from which the transaction is copied is written in the post. ref. column. The abbreviation "P" precedes the page number, to show that the entry came from the purchases journal.

(5) POST. REF. COLUMN OF PURCHASES JOURNAL COMPLETED. Finally, a check is placed in the accounts payable subsidiary ledger account.

The following example of a creditor's account in the account payable ledger shows posting of the above purchases journal entry of a $512 purchase. Note that an earlier $100 purchase had already been entered in the account, and that the new credit balance is now $612.

Harris Supply Co.
14 West Street, Chicago, Ill.

DATE		ITEM	POST REF.	DEBIT	CREDIT	CREDIT BALANCE
198— Jan	4		P4		1 00 00	
	10		P6		5 1 2 00	6 1 2 00

b. MONTH-END TOTALING. At the end of the month, the purchase journal is totaled and ruled. This is done by adding up all the entries in the amount column, drawing a single line, writing the totaled below this single line, and then drawing a double line below the total.

44

DATE 198__		FROM WHOM PURCHASED	POST REF.	AMOUNT
Jan	10	Harris Supply	✓	512 00
	12	Rich Co.	✓	100 00
	15	Poor Co.	✓	50 00
	25	Broke Corp.	✓	50 00
	29	G. R. T. Co.	✓	258 00
	31			970 00
				(512) (270)

Purchases Journal   Page 6

The above example shows the purchases journal after it has been totaled and ruled. (The numbers in parentheses under the total refer to purchases and accounts payable controlling ledger accounts, and are placed there after total has been posted to those accounts. See below.)

c. MONTH-END POSTING TO GENERAL LEDGER PURCHASES ACCOUNT. The month-end total of the purchases journal is posted to the purchases account in the general ledger. The purchases account is *debited* with the month-end total. The amount is entered in the debit column, then the date and post. ref. (purchases journal page number). Finally, the number of the purchases account in the general ledger (512 in the above example) is written in parentheses under the total column of the purchases journal. This shows that the total has been posted to the purchases account.

Purchases   Account #512

DATE	ITEM	POST REF.	DEBIT	DATE	ITEM	POST REF.	CREDIT
198__ Jan 31		P6	970 00				

End of Month Posting from Purchase Journal to General Ledger Purchase Account

d. MONTH-END POSTING TO THE GENERAL LEDGER ACCOUNTS PAYABLE CONTROLLING ACCOUNT. The month-end total of the purchases journal is posted to the accounts payable controlling account in the general ledger. It is *credited* to the account. (Note that this single credit represents the sum of all the individual credits that have been entered day by day during the month into the individual creditor accounts in the accounts payable ledger. In this way, we see how the accounts payable controlling account in the general ledger summarizes or controls its subsidiary accounts payable ledger.)

An example of month-end posting from the purchases journal to the general ledger accounts payable controlling account follows. The amount—$970—is written in the credit column, then date and post. ref. column are completed. (The post. ref. column shows the page of the purchases journal from which the entry was copied.) Finally, the number of the accounts payable controlling account (220 in this example) would be written below the total in the purchases journal, in parentheses. This number indicates that posting to the account has been done.

DATE	ITEM	POST REF	DEBIT	DATE	ITEM	POST REF	CREDIT
				¹98⁻ Jan 31		P6	9 70 00

Month-End Posting from Purchase Journal to General Ledger Accounts
Payable Controlling Account

SUMMARY

The following points should be remembered in connection with use of the purchases journal.

1. All merchandise purchased on account is journalized in the purchases journal, not in the general journal.
2. Daily posting is made from the purchases journal to the individual creditor accounts in the accounts payable subsidiary ledger. Each account is credited.
3. At the month's end, the purchases journal is totaled and ruled. The total is debited to the purchases account in the general ledger, and credited to the accounts payable controlling account in the general ledger.

Specialized Journals: The Cash Receipts Journal | 15

In many business transactions, cash is received. For example, cash is received when a cash sale is made, when a customer pays his outstanding bill, when the firm borrows money from a bank, etc., and from other miscellaneous sources. The cash may be in the form of currency or in the form of a check.

JOURNALIZING CASH RECEIPTS

Every time cash is received, the company's cash account is increased. As we know, when an asset (such as cash) is increased, this is shown by *debiting* the account. Therefore, every time a transaction involving the receipt of cash occurs, the cash account is debited.

USE OF MULTI-COLUMNAR JOURNAL FOR RECORDING CASH RECEIPTS

When a transaction involving receipt of cash occurs, there will be a journal entry debiting the cash account. In Chapter 9, on the multi-columnar journal, we saw one method of simplifying journalizing

and posting of all these cash debits through the use of a multi-columnar journal with special columns for cash debits and cash credits.

CASH RECEIPTS JOURNAL

There is another method for simplifying the journalizing of all these cash debits that occur every time cash is received. This involves recording all transactions where cash is received in a special journal—the *cash receipts journal*—rather than in the general journal.

1. **Description of Cash Receipts Journal.** One form of cash receipts journal provides columns for listing the date of the transaction, the name of the account to be credited, and a post. ref. column in which the ledger account, to which the transaction is later posted, can be identified. There are also four columns in which the amount can be written, depending on the transaction. There are three credit columns—sales credit, accounts receivable credit and miscellaneous credit. There is one debit column—cash debit.

\multicolumn{8}{c|}{Cash Receipts Journal — Page 7}							
DATE	ACCOUNT CREDITED	POST REF.	MISCELLANEOUS CREDIT	SALES CREDIT	ACCTS REC CREDIT	CASH DEBIT	

This is just one example of a cash receipts journal page. Depending on the needs of the business, as many other credit or debit columns may be added as are required. (See Chapter 20 for other examples of cash receipts journal.)

2. **Journalizing a Cash Receipt Transaction.** Each time cash is received by a business firm, some record of the transaction is sent to the bookkeeper—perhaps a cash register tape or the check itself, etc. Working from this business document, the bookkeeper journalizes the transaction on *one line* of the cash receipts journal.

a. DATE. The bookkeeper enters the date of the transaction in the date column.

b. ACCOUNT. The name of the account which provided the cash is entered in the account column.

  (1) If cash came from cash sales, then "sales" is written in the account column.

  (2) If cash came from payment by a customer of his bill, then the customer's name is written in the account column.

  (3) If cash came from a miscellaneous source such as interest on a bank ac-

count at First National Bank, or income from subleasing part of the plant, then the name of this account is written in account column (interest income, rent income, etc.).

c. POST. REF. This column is left blank for the time being. It will be completed later when journal entry is posted to ledger.

d. CREDIT COLUMN. The amount of the transaction is written in whichever *one* of the credit columns it belongs. The amount of cash *sale* would be written in the *sale* credit column. The amount of a payment by a customer of his *account* would be written in the *accounts payable* credit column. All other items would be entered in the miscellaneous credit column.

e. CASH DEBIT COLUMN. *In every case, the amount is also written in the cash debit column.*

EXAMPLES. The following examples show how three typical transactions involving receipt of cash would be journalized in the cash receipt journal.

On January 10th, the company received $100 in cash from cash sales. The item is entered in the sales credit column and the cash debit column. Whenever a sale entry is made, a check is written in the post. ref. column at the same time. This indicates that separate posting of this sale is not necessary—since the total of the *sales* column is posted to the sales account at the end of the month.

		Cash Receipts Journal					Page 7	
DATE		ACCOUNT CREDITED	POST REF	MISC. CREDIT	SALES CREDIT	ACCTS. REC. CREDIT	CASH DEBIT	
Jan 10		Sales	✓		100 00		100 00	

On January 14th, the company received a check in the mail for $200 in payment of Brown Company's account. The amount is entered in the account receivable credit column and in the cash debit column.

		Cash Receipts Journal					Page 7	
DATE		ACCOUNT CREDITED	POST REF	MISC. CREDIT	SALES CREDIT	ACCTS. REC. CREDIT	CASH DEBIT	
Jan 10		Sales			100 00		100 00	
14		H Brown Co				200 00	200 00	

On January 21st, the company received a check in the mail for $50 from a tenant to whom it subleases part of its office space. The amount is listed in the account column as "rent income," and is entered in the miscellaneous credit column and the cash debit column.

		Cash Receipts Journal					Page 7	
DATE		ACCOUNT CREDITED	POST REF	MISC. CREDIT	SALES CREDIT	ACCTS. REC. CREDIT	CASH DEBIT	
Jan 10		Sales			100 00		100 00	
14		H Brown Co				200 00	200 00	
21		Rent Income		50 00			50 00	

POSTING FROM THE CASH RECEIPTS JOURNAL

Posting from the cash receipts journal to the ledger involves several procedures.

1. **Daily Posting of Accounts Receivable Credits.** It is important that the firm know at all times the amount of money each individual customer owes it. Therefore, the individual customer accounts in the accounts receivable ledger must be kept up to date. To do this, it is advisable to arrange for *daily (or very frequent) posting of all amounts entered as credits in the accounts receivable credit column* of the cash receipts journal. Each of these amounts should be posted daily as a credit to the individual customer's account in the accounts receivable ledger.
   a. LOCATE CUSTOMER'S ACCOUNT. In the accounts receivable ledger, find the account of the customer whose account has been credited in the cash receipts journal.
   b. ENTER AMOUNT IN CREDIT COLUMN. Enter the amount in the credit column of the cus-

tomer's account. Compute and enter the new debit balance in the customer's account.
   c. ENTER DATE.
   d. COMPLETE POST. REF. COLUMN IN CUSTOMER'S ACCOUNT. Write the page number of the cash receipts journal page from which the transaction has been posted. Precede page number with the initials "CR" to show that the transaction was originally journalized in the cash receipts journal.
   e. COMPLETE POST. REF. COLUMN OF THE CASH RECEIPTS JOURNAL. Place a checkmark in the post. ref. column of the cash receipts journal on the line where the transaction was journalized. This shows that the transaction has been posted to the individual customer account.

Below is an illustration of H. Brown Company's account in the accounts receivable ledger. The January 14th journal credit entry of $200 from the cash receipts journal has been posted to the Brown account. Note the new debit balance of $300 resulting after crediting Brown's account with $200.

H. Brown Co
14 Avon Street - Ames, Ohio

DATE	ITEM	POST REF	DEBIT	CREDIT	DEBIT BALANCE
198– Jan 8		S2	500 00		
14		CR7		200 00	300 00

2. **Posting of Miscellaneous Credit Items.** From time to time during the month the bookkeeper will post each entry in the *miscellaneous credit column* to its appropriate ledger account. For example, we saw how cash received from rent income was listed as a credit in the miscellaneous credit column. To post this, these steps are followed:
   a. LOCATE RENT INCOME ACCOUNT. Locate the rent income account in the general ledger.
   b. ENTER AMOUNT ON CREDIT SIDE. Enter the amount in the rent income, *on the credit side of the ledger*.
   c. ENTER DATE.
   d. COMPLETE POST. REF. COLUMN OF RENT INCOME ACCOUNT. Enter the number of the page of the cash receipts journal from which

you are posting into the post. ref. column of the ledger account. Use the letters "CR" to indicate that you are posting from cash receipts journal.
   e. COMPLETE POST. REF. COLUMN OF CASH RECEIPTS JOURNAL. Write the *number* of the account which you have just posted in the post. ref. column of the cash receipts journal. This shows that the miscellaneous credit entry has been posted.

An illustration of the rent income general ledger account follows, showing how the January 21st entry in the cash receipts journal was posted to the account. The credit of $50.00 has been credited to this rent income account.

DATE	ITEM	POST REF	DEBIT	DATE	ITEM	POST REF	CREDIT
				198– Jan 25		CR7	50 00

Rent Income · Account #425

3. Totaling of Cash Receipts Journal. At the end of the month, all the columns in the cash receipts book are totaled. The bookkeeper checks to make sure that the total of the cash debit column equals the total of the three credit columns (sales, accounts receivable and miscellaneous). A double line is drawn below the totals. A check is placed under total in the miscellaneous column to show that these items have been posted individually and no further posting is needed.

Cash Receipts Journal   Page 7

DATE	ACCOUNT CREDITED	POST REF	MISC. CREDIT	SALES CREDIT	ACCTS. REC CREDIT	CASH DEBIT
198– Jan 10	Sales	✓		100 00		100 00
14	H. Brown Co.	✓			200 00	200 00
21	Rent Income	425	50 00			50 00
22	B. Love Corp.	✓			75 00	75 00
26	Jack and Co	✓			25 00	25 00
27	Sales	✓		50 00		50 00
31			50 00	150 00	300 00	500 00

4. Posting the Sales Credit Column Total. The month-end *total* of the sales credit column is then posted by *crediting* the sales account in the *general ledger*. Below is an illustration of the general ledger sales account, showing how the month-end total of $150.00 in the sales column of the cash receipts journal has been posted.

DATE	ITEM	POST REF	DEBIT	DATE 198–		POST REF	CREDIT
				Jan 31		CR7	150 00

Sales · Account #410

After the sales account in the general ledger has been posted, the number of this sales account (410) is written in parentheses below the double line under the total of the sales credit column in the cash receipts ledger. This shows that posting has been completed.

5. Posting the Accounts Receivable Credit Column Total. The month-end total of the accounts receivable credit column is posted (credited) to the accounts receivable controlling account in the general ledger. Here we see how the total from the accounts receivable credit column—$300.00—has been posted to the general ledger accounts receivable controlling account.

DATE	ITEM	POST REF.	DEBIT	DATE 198_	ITEM	POST REF.	CREDIT
				Jan 31		CR7	3 0 0 00

Accounts Receivable — Account #120

After the accounts receivable controlling account has been posted, the number of the account is written in parentheses under the column total in the cash receipts journal, to show that posting has been completed.

6. Posting the Cash Debit Column Total. The month-end total of the cash debit column is posted (debited) to the cash account in the general ledger. Here we see how the cash debit total—$500.00—was posted to the cash account in the general ledger.

Cash — Account #110

DATE 198_	ITEM	POST REF.	DEBIT	DATE	ITEM	POST REF.	CREDIT
Jan 31		CR7	5 0 0 00				

After posting the cash account, the number of the account (110 in this example) is written in parentheses under the cash debit column in the cash receipts ledger to show that posting has been completed.

SUMMARY OF POSTING PROCEDURES FROM CASH RECEIPTS JOURNALS

1. Post credits daily to individual accounts in the accounts receivable ledger.
2. Fairly frequently during the month, post individual credits in the miscellaneous credit column to appropriate general ledger accounts.
3. At the end of the month, total all the columns and check to see if the total of all credit columns equals the total in the cash debit column.
4. Post the total in the accounts receivable credit column as a credit to the general ledger accounts receivable controlling account.
5. Post the total in the sales column as a credit to the sales account in the general ledger.
6. Post the total in the cash column as a debit to the cash account in the general ledger.

Specialized Journals: The Cash Payments Journal | 16

CASH PAYMENTS

Many business transactions involve the payment of cash by the business. (When payment of *cash* is made in a business situation, *either* currency or check is meant; however most business transactions involving payment of cash by a business *are made by check*.) For example, cash payments take place when a bill for merchandise or equipment is paid, when wages or rent are paid, etc. Procedures for writing and recording checks and currency payments are discussed in more detail in Chapter 23.

JOURNALIZING CASH PAYMENTS

Every time cash is paid out by a company, the cash account is reduced. To show the decrease of the asset account cash, we *credit the cash account*. Therefore, every time a cash payment is made, the transaction is journalized as a credit to cash, and a debit to the other account involved.

JOURNALS FOR USE IN JOURNALIZING CASH PAYMENTS

It is possible to journalize all cash payments in the general 2-column journal, and this is sometimes done by very small firms. We also saw in Chapter 9 how a 4-column journal could be used to simplify the journalizing of such a transaction. In such a 4-column journal, a special cash credit column is provided to list all cash credits.

Many businesses, however, prefer to use a *separate* journal, the cash payments journal, to journalize all transactions involving the payment of cash.

CASH PAYMENTS JOURNAL

A cash payments journal is a special journal or book of original entry used only for the journalizing of transactions involving payments of cash.

1. **Description.** The specific form of a cash payments journal will vary with the needs of the particular business. In general, columns are provided for listing the date, account to be debited as a result of the cash payment, the number of the check issued, and post. ref. Several debit columns are provided in order to group various kinds of payments. A typical cash payments journal, for example, might include special debit columns for accounts payable debits, salary expense debits and miscellaneous debits. A single *cash credit* column is provided.

Cash Payments Journal							Page 4	
DATE	ACCOUNT DEBITED	CHECK NO	POST REF	GENERAL DEBIT	ACCTS PAYABLE DEBIT	SALARY EXPENSE DEBIT	CASH CREDIT	

2. **Journalizing a Cash Payments Transaction.** When a cash payment is made, some record of it is sent to the bookkeeper, perhaps a form (called a *voucher*), which indicates that a payment has been authorized and made. Working from this original business paper, the bookkeeper will journalize the transaction on one line of the cash payments journal.

a. DATE. Date on which payment was made will be entered in the date column.
b. ACCOUNT. The name of the ledger account for which the cash has been paid is entered in the *account debited* column. For example:
   (1) If the payment was made to a creditor in payment of an outstanding bill, the

creditor's name is written in the account column;

    (2) If the payment was made to cover one of the expenses of the business, i.e., rent or insurance or office supplies, etc., then the name of this ledger account (rent expense, insurance expense, office expense, etc.) is written in the account column;

    (3) If the payment was made to a bank to pay off a loan, then the name of the bank loan account, notes payable, would be written in the account column;

    (4) If the cash payment represented a withdrawal of cash from the business by one of the proprietors, then "drawing account" is listed in the account column.

c. CHECK NUMBER. Checks come in a book or folder and are numbered in order. The number of the check used to make the payment involved in this transaction is written in this column.

d. POST. REF. When the entry is posted to the ledgers, this column will be completed.

e. DEBIT COLUMNS. The amount of the transaction will be written in whichever one of the debit columns to which it belongs. For example, the cash payments journal illustrated here has an accounts payable debit column. Therefore, cash payments to creditors are listed in this column. This cash payments journal also has a salary expense column. Therefore, payments for salaries would be entered in the salary expense debit column. All other items for which no special debit columns have been provided, are entered in the general debit column. (In some cash payments journals, *general* debit column is called *miscellaneous* debit or *sundry* debit.)

f. CASH CREDIT COLUMN. The amount of *every* transaction is *also written in the cash credit column.*

EXAMPLES. The following examples show how typical transactions of the Saul Company involving payment of cash might be journalized in Saul Company's cash payments journal.

On November 9th, using check number 415, the Saul Company paid a bill for $50, which it owed to The Boat Supply Corp. The date is entered in the date column, Boat Supply Corp. is written in the account debited column. The check number, 415, is entered in check number column. This payment is to reduce one of Saul Company's *accounts payable,* so the amount is entered in the accounts payable debit column. It is also entered in the cash credit column.

Cash Payments Journal   Page 4

DATE	ACCOUNT DEBITED	CHECK NO.	POST REF	GENERAL DEBIT	ACCOUNTS PAYABLE DEBIT	SALARY EXPENSE DEBIT	CASH CREDIT
198— Nov. 9	Boat Supply Corp.	415			50 00		50 00

On November 14th, using check number 416, Saul Company paid the monthly rent of $200. The date is recorded. Rent expense is written in the account debited column, and the check number is recorded.

Since there is *no* special debit column for rent expense, it is entered in the *general* debit column. It is also entered in cash credit column.

Cash Payments Journal   Page 4

DATE	ACCOUNT DEBITED	CHECK NO.	POST REF	GENERAL DEBIT	ACCOUNTS PAYABLE DEBIT	SALARY EXPENSE DEBIT	CASH CREDIT
198— Nov. 9	Boat Supply Corp.	415			50 00		50 00
14	Rent Expense	416		200 00			200 00

On November 29th Saul Company paid salaries of $250 with check number 417. The date, account debited (salary expense) and check number are entered. The amount is entered in the special *salary expense debit column,* and in the cash credit column.

DATE		ACCOUNT DEBITED	CHECK #	POST. REF.	GENERAL DEBIT	ACCOUNTS PAYABLE DEBIT	SALARY EXPENSE DEBIT	CASH CREDIT
198- Nov	9	Boat Supply Corp	415			50 00		50 00
	14	Rent Expense	416		200 00			200 00
	29	Salary Expense	417	✓			250 00	250 00

The student should note that each time a salary expense item is journalized, a check is placed in the post. ref. column to show that no further posting of this *individual* item is necessary. A salary expense column has been provided, and a *total* salary expense figure will be posted at the month's end.

On November 29th, Mr. G. Saul, the proprietor, made a withdrawal of $400 from the firm. The date, name of the account to be debited (G. Saul, Drawing) and check number are recorded. The amount is listed in the *general debit* column since there is no special drawing account debit column. It is also listed in the cash credit column.

Cash Payments Journal   Page 4

DATE		ACCOUNT DEBITED	CHECK #	POST. REF.	GENERAL DEBIT	ACCOUNTS PAYABLE DEBIT	SALARY EXPENSE DEBIT	CASH CREDIT
198- Nov	9	Boat Supply Corp	415			50 00		50 00
	14	Rent Expense	416		200 00			200 00
	29	Salary Expense	417	✓			250 00	250 00
	29	G. Saul, Drawing	418		400 00			400 00

3. Posting From Cash Payments Journal to Individual Customer Accounts. Posting from the cash payments journal involves several procedures.

a. FREQUENT POSTING OF INDIVIDUAL ACCOUNTS PAYABLE DEBITS. It is important that the firm have a current record of how much it owes each creditor. For that reason, very frequent posting of the payments made to creditors (which are listed in the accounts payable debit column) should be done from the cash payments journal to the individual creditor's accounts in the accounts payable ledger. Many firms do this daily.

(1) LOCATE INDIVIDUAL CREDITOR ACCOUNT. For each item listed in the accounts payable debit column, locate the individual creditor account in the accounts payable ledger.

(2) POST THE AMOUNT FROM THE CASH PAYMENTS JOURNAL TO DEBIT SIDE OF CREDITOR'S ACCOUNT. Enter the amount in the *debit* column of the creditor's account. Compute and enter the new credit balance (if any) in the account.

(3) ENTER DATE.

(4) COMPLETE POST. REF. COLUMN OF CREDITOR'S ACCOUNT. In the post. ref. column write the initials CP and the page number of the cash payment journal from which the item was posted.

b. COMPLETE POST. REF. COLUMN OF CASH PAYMENTS JOURNAL. Put a check in the post. ref. column of the cash payments journal, on the line from which you have copied this entry. This shows that posting to the individual creditor's account has been completed.

An illustration of The Boat Supply Corp. account in the Saul Company accounts payable ledger follows, showing posting of a cash payment of $50 from the cash payments ledger.

Boat Supply Corp.
300 Central Ave. Boston, Mass.

DATE		ITEMS	POST REF	DEBIT	CREDIT	CREDIT BALANCE
198– Nov.	1		P7		200 00	200 00
	9		CP4	50 00		150 00

4. Posting of Items Recorded in the General Debit Column. During the month, from time to time, the bookkeeper will post a debit for each entry for which an amount was recorded in the general debit column. Each amount will be posted as a *debit* to the ledger account debited column.

For example, we saw how the November 14th entry of $200 of rent expense was recorded in the general debit column of the cash payments journal. At some time during the month, the bookkeeper would follow the procedure outlined here.

a. LOCATE RENT EXPENSE LEDGER CARD.

b. POST THE AMOUNT. Post the amount—$200—on the debit side of the ledger account, rent expense.

c. COMPLETE DATE AND POST. REF. COLUMNS OF LEDGER ACCOUNT. Enter the date of the transaction (Nov. 14th) and the page number of the journal (CP 4) in the ledger account.

d. COMPLETE POST. REF. COLUMN ON JOURNAL. Write the number of the rent expense ledger account—540 in this example—in the post. ref. column of the cash payments journal.

The following example shows how the $200 entry was posted to the ledger account—rent expense.

Rent Expense   Account #540

DATE		ITEMS	POST REF	DEBIT	DATE	ITEMS	POST REF	CREDIT
198– Nov.	14		CP4	200 00				

The following example shows how another general debit entry, the $400 debit to G. Saul, Drawing, was posted to the G. Saul Drawing account in the general ledger. The number of this account, 350, would be written in the post. ref. column of the journal on the line from which the entry was posted.

G. Saul, Drawing   Account #350

DATE		ITEMS	POST REF	DEBIT	DATE	ITEMS	POST REF	CREDIT
198– Nov.	30		CP4	400 00				

5. Month-End Totaling of Cash Payments Journal. We have seen how the accounts payable and general debit columns are posted from time to time during the month. At the end of the month, all the columns in the cash payment journals are totaled. A check is made to see if the total of all the debit columns equals the total of the credit column. If so, a double line is drawn under the totals. A check is placed below the general debit column to indicate that each of the entries in this column has been posted individually, and that no further posting of general debit entries is necessary.

DATE	ACCOUNT DEBITED	CHECK #	POST REF	GENERAL DEBIT	ACCOUNTS PAYABLE DEBIT	SALARY EXPENSE DEBIT	CASH CREDIT
198— Nov. 19	Boat Supply Corp.	415	✓		50 00		50 00
24	Rent Expense	416	540	200 00			200 00
29	Salary Expense	417				250 00	250 00
29	G. Saul, Drawing	418	350	400 00			400 00
29	Ethel Co.	419	✓		100 00		100 00
29	C. Henig	420	✓		50 00		50 00
30	Salary Expense	421	✓			50 00	50 00
				600 00	200 00	300 00	1100 00
				(✓)	(210)	(540)	(110)

Note in this example that the total of the debit columns (600 + 200 + 300) equals the total of the credit column (1100).

6. **Posting of Column Totals.** All column totals except the general debit column are now posted.

a. POSTING ACCOUNTS PAYABLE DEBIT TO-TAL. The total in the accounts payable debit column is posted by *debiting* the accounts payable controlling account in the general ledger. Below we see how month-end posting of the $200 total is done.

Accounts Payable								Account #210	
DATE	ITEMS	POST REF	DEBIT	DATE	ITEMS	POST REF	CREDIT		
198— Nov. 30		CP4	200 00						

After this posting has been completed, the number of the accounts payable controlling account in the general ledger (210 in our example) is written in parentheses below the total of the accounts payable debit column in the cash payments journal. This indicates that posting of the total has been completed.

b. POSTING SALARY EXPENSE DEBIT TOTAL. The month-end total of the salary expense debit column (or of any other special debit column which a cash payments journal happens to have) is posted as a *debit* to the appropriate general ledger account. Here we see how the total of the salary expense debit column ($300) is posted as a debit to the salary expense account.

Salary Expense								Account #540	
DATE	ITEMS	POST REF	DEBIT	DATE	ITEMS	POST REF	CREDIT		
198— Nov. 30		CP4	300 00						

After posting the salary expense debit account, write the number of the account (540 in the example) below the total of the salary expense column in the cash payments journal. This indicates that posting of the total has been completed.

c. POSTING THE CASH CREDIT COLUMN. The month-end total of the cash credit column is posted as a *credit* to the cash account.

				Cash			Account #110	

DATE	ITEMS	POST REF	DEBIT	DATE	ITEMS	POST REF	CREDIT
				198– Nov. 30		CP4	1100 00

After crediting the cash account, write the number of the cash account below the double line under the cash credit column total to show that posting of this column has been completed.

SUMMARY

In many businesses, a cash payments journal is used to record transactions involving cash payments. Usually, cash payments are made by check and the check stub (or a cash voucher) is sent to the bookkeeper to record the transaction. Each transaction is journalized by entering the amount in the cash credit column and in the appropriate debit column.

The bookkeeper does frequent posting, during the month, of individual debits entered in the accounts payable debit column and the general debit column. At the month's end, she totals all the columns and checks to see if the total of the debit columns equals the total of the credit column. She then posts the totals of all the columns except the general debit column. The total of each special debit column is posted as a debit to its appropriate general ledger account (i.e., accounts payable to accounts payable controlling account; salary expense to salary expense account, etc.). The total of the cash credit is posted as a credit to the cash account.

Combination Journal 17

VARIOUS KINDS OF JOURNAL SYSTEMS

Depending on the need of the business, there are various kinds of journal systems which may prove satisfactory. For example, we saw in Chapter 8 how a simple 2- or 4-column journal could be used for journalizing all transactions in a relatively small business. Chapters 13 through 16 explained the use of a system of individual specialized journals along with a general journal, this system being appropriate for larger enterprises. The *combination journal* discussed in this chapter provides another kind of journal system.

COMBINATION JOURNAL

The combination journal is a single book of entry used for journalizing transactions of a business. It provides special *columns* for segregating many of the entries for which separate *books* are provided when a system of specialized journals is used. We have noted that use of a system of specialized journals permits several bookkeepers to journalize at once—when a single combination journal is used, only one person can work on the journal at one time.

Occasionally, a combination journal is used by a firm in combination with a general journal in which the closing and adjusting entries are recorded.

EXAMPLE OF COMBINATION JOURNAL

A typical combination journal might include many different columns. As in all journals, columns are provided for listing the date, name of account and post. ref. In addition, the following account columns might be provided for segregating different categories of entries:

a. Cash debit and cash credit columns.
b. Accounts receivable debit and accounts receivable credit columns.
c. Accounts payable debit column and accounts payable credit column.
d. Purchases debit and sales credit columns.
e. A general debit and general credit column for items not covered in the above categories.

A column might also be provided, perhaps, for listing check numbers of all checks written by the company in connection with payments or withdrawals.

By using these special columns to record individual entries, the bookkeeper can have readily available summarized totals of the most common ledger account items. This simplifies posting, since in many cases it is only necessary to post month-end *column totals*, rather than individual entries. For example, if a combination journal has a separate sales credit column, it is only necessary to post the month-end sales credit column as a credit to the sales ledger account, rather than to post each individual sale during the month.

1. **Journalizing in the Combination Journal.** Each transaction of the business is recorded in the combination journal. Debits and credits are entered either in a special debit or credit column, or in the general debit or credit column if no appropriate special column has been provided. As each transaction is journalized, the date is written in the date column in the usual manner. A few examples of journal entries in this type of a combination journal follow.

a. MERCHANDISE SOLD ON CREDIT. When merchandise is sold on credit, the customer's name is written in the "name of account" column. A sale on account is journalized by debiting accounts receivable and crediting sales, so the amount is entered in the accounts receivable debit column and the sales credit column. This is illustrated in the combination journal shown here by the May 2nd sale of $25 to Herb Manel.

b. CUSTOMER PAYS HIS BILL. When a customer pays his bill, the customer's name is written in the "name of account" column. A payment of an accounts receivable is journalized by crediting accounts receivable and debiting cash, so the amount is entered in the cash debit column and the accounts receivable credit column (see May 4th entry).

c. FIRM BUYS MERCHANDISE ON ACCOUNT. The name of the seller of the merchandise (the creditor) is written in the "name of account" column. We know that a purchase on account is journalized by debiting purchases and crediting accounts payable, so the amount is entered in the purchase debit column and the accounts payable credit column. We see this in the May 12th entry in the combination journal showing the purchase by our company of $100 worth of merchandise on account from the Hayes Hat Company.

d. FIRM PAYS A CREDITOR'S ACCOUNT. The name of the creditor is written in the "name of account" column. A payment of an outstanding account payable is journalized by debiting accounts payable and crediting cash, so the amount is entered in the accounts payable debit and cash credit columns. The check number of the check used to pay the creditor is written in the check number column. For example, the May 22nd entry shows payment made to Hayes Hat Company with check number 2247.

e. FIRM PAYS EXPENSES. When expenses, such as rent expense or salary expense, are paid, the expense account is debited and the cash account is credited. The name of the expense account is written in the "name of accounts" column (i.e., rent expense). The amount is entered in the *general debit* column (since there is no rent expense debit column) and in the cash credit column. The check number of the check used to pay the rent expense is written in the check number column. On May 29th we see journal entries showing payment of $50 of rent expense with check number 2248.

f. PURCHASES OF EQUIPMENT, SUPPLIES OR OTHER NON-MERCHANDISE ITEMS. When equipment, etc., is purchased by a firm on account, the equipment account is debited and the account of the creditor who sold the equipment is credited. Two lines will be needed to journalize this transaction. On the first line, the name of the account to be debited—equipment—will be written. The amount is entered in the *general debit* column (since there is no equipment debit column). On the second line, the name of the creditor is written, and the amount is entered in the accounts payable credit column. Purchases of supplies or other non-merchandise items would be handled similarly. See May 31st entry in combination journal showing purchase of $75.00 of equipment from Green Supply Company.

g. CASH SALES. Cash sales are entered by writing *sales* in the name of account column. A cash sale results in an increase in cash, so cash account is debited, and sales account is credited. This is shown by entering the amount in the cash debit column and in the sales credit column. See May 31st entry.

h. JOURNALIZING OTHER TRANSACTIONS. From time to time the bookkeeper will be confronted with other kinds of transactions to journalize. If a special column is provided in the journal for at least one of the specific accounts affected by the transaction, then only one line will be needed to journalize it. If not, two lines will be required. In all cases, the debits and credits are recorded either in a special debit or credit column if one has been provided, or in the general debit or credit columns if not.

2. **Posting From the Combination Journal.**

a. POSTING GENERAL CREDIT AND GENERAL DEBIT ITEMS. *Each of the entries listed in the general debit or general credit columns must be posted individually to its respective ledger account, as shown in the "name of account" column.* This is done at intervals during the month. For example, the combination journal illustrated here shows that on May 29th the bookkeeper recorded a $50 item, rent expense, in the general debit column. This $50 must be posted as a debit to the rent expense account in the general ledger. After posting, the number of the rent expense account is written in the post. ref. column of the combination journal to show that posting has been completed. Continuing along in the combination journal, the bookkeeper would do similar individual posting of each item listed in the general debit and general credit columns.

b. POSTING TO THE INDIVIDUAL ACCOUNTS IN THE SUBSIDIARY ACCOUNTS PAYABLE AND ACCOUNTS RECEIVABLE LEDGERS. *Each item entered in the debit or credit columns for accounts payable or accounts receivable must be posted individually (at frequent intervals during the month) to the individual account in the accounts payable or accounts receivable ledger. Amounts entered in the accounts receivable debit column are posted as a debit to the individual customer account whose name appears in the "name of account" column.* For example, the May 2nd debit in the accounts receivable column should be posted as a debit to Herb Manel's account in the accounts receivable subsidiary ledger. After this posting is completed, a check mark is placed in the post. ref. column of the combination journal to show that posting has been completed.

Similar procedures would be followed for every other item listed in accounts receivable debit and credit columns and the accounts payable debit and credit columns. For example, the May 12th accounts payable credit would be posted as a credit to the Hayes Hat account in the accounts payable ledger, and the May 22nd accounts payable debit would be posted as a debit to Hayes Hat.

c. TOTALING THE COLUMNS AT THE END OF THE ACCOUNTING PERIOD. At the end of the accounting period (probably at the month's end), all the columns in the combination journal are footed. The totals of all the credit columns are added together to see if their sum matches the sum total of all the debit columns. If so, double lines are ruled.

d. POSTING COLUMN TOTALS. The total of each of the columns, except *the general debit and general credit columns*, is posted as a debit or credit to the account as shown by the column title. For example, accounts payable debit column total is posted as a debit to the accounts payable controlling account, and the accounts payable credit column total is posted as a credit to the accounts payable controlling account. Similarly, the sales credit column total is posted as a credit to sales account, etc.

The number of the general ledger account to which the amount has been posted is written in parentheses below the double line of each column total. A check is placed below the double line under the general debit and general credit columns to show that no further posting is required.

Combination Journal   Page 10

CASH DEBIT	CASH CREDIT	CHECK NO.	DATE	NAME OF ACCOUNT	POST REF	GENERAL DEBIT	GENERAL CREDIT	ACCOUNTS PAYABLE DEBIT	ACCOUNTS PAYABLE CREDIT	ACCOUNTS RECEIVABLE DEBIT	ACCOUNTS RECEIVABLE CREDIT	PURCHASES DEBIT	SALES CREDIT
			May 2	Herb Manel	✓					25 00			25 00
40 00			4	Ed Vide	✓						40 00		
			12	Hayes Hat	✓				100 00			100 00	
	100 00	2247	22	Hayes Hat	✓			100 00					
	50 00	2248	29	Rent Expense	525	50 00							
			31	Equipment	130	75 00							
				Screen Supply Co.	✓				75 00				
150 00				Sales	✓								150 00
190 00	150 00		31			125 00		100 00	175 00	25 00	40 00	100 00	175 00
(110)	(110)					(✓)	(✓)	(210)	(210)	(120)	(120)	(510)	(410)

Capital Accounts in a Proprietorship | 18

OPENING THE PROPRIETORSHIP ACCOUNT

In a business run by a single proprietor (single proprietorship) the original ownership interest in the business is shown by a credit in the proprietorship account. The proprietorship account is usually called the *capital* account. For example, assume Mr. Robert Robbins wishes to open a barber shop. He borrows $5000 from the bank, invests $2000 of his own money, buys $6000 worth of equipment and has $1000 in cash left. His balance sheet would show:

Assets		Liabilities	
Cash	$1000	Bank loan	$5000
Equipment	6000		
		Proprietorship	
		Robert Robbins, capital	$2000

In the ledger, there would be a Robert Robbins capital account which would show a credit balance of $2000, indicating Mr. Robbins' investment or proprietorship interest in the business.

						Robert Robbins, Capital				#301	
DATE	ITEM		POST REF	DEBIT	DATE	ITEM		POST REF	CREDIT		
					198— Jan 1			J1	2000 00		

PERMANENT CHANGES IN THE CAPITAL ACCOUNT

From time to time there may be permanent changes in the capital account. As the business shows signs of growing, the proprietor may invest additional *permanent* funds. Or, the proprietor may decide to withdraw funds on a *permanent* basis and operate the business with a smaller investment. These permanent changes in capital (which should *not* be confused with temporary changes discussed below) are reflected directly in the *capital account in the ledger.*

For example, if Mr. Robbins wishes to invest an additional $1000 permanently in the business, a journal entry would be made debiting cash $1000 (to show the increase in cash) and crediting Robert Robbins, capital account (to show the increase in the proprietorship account). After posting, Robert Robbins' capital account would show this:

						Robert Robbins, Capital				#301	
DATE	ITEM		POST REF	DEBIT	DATE	ITEM		POST REF	CREDIT		
					198— Jan 1			J1	2000 00		
					Sept. 1			CR5	1000 00		

A permanent reduction in the capital account would take place if, at a later date, Mr. Robbins decided to withdraw $1500 in cash from the business, and operate the business *permanently* with this decreased capital. The cash account would be credited to show decrease in cash in the business, and the Robert Robbins capital account would be debited to show the decrease in the proprietorship account.

TEMPORARY CHANGES IN CAPITAL ACCOUNTS

Most changes in capital accounts, however, are not of a permanent nature. During the year a business will earn profits, which will increase the proprietor's interest in the business. Also, during the year the proprietor will withdraw sums of money from this business for his own personal use. These are withdrawals made in anticipation of profits or from current profits, rather than withdrawals made to reduce permanently the investment in the business. In other words, the profits earned during the year and the withdrawals made during the year are not necessarily increases or decreases in the capital that will remain permanently in the business. Therefore, these increases and decreases are not recorded directly in the *capital account*. Instead, they are recorded in a separate proprietorship account called the *proprietor's drawing account*.

1. **Withdrawals.** During the year, when the proprietor withdraws money from the business for his own personal use, such withdrawals are shown by *debiting the proprietor's drawing account*. For example, every week, Mr. Robbins withdraws $100 for his own personal use. Jour-

nal entries would show a credit to cash (since the business' cash is decreased) and a *debit to R. Robbins, drawing account.*

2. **Temporary Increases in Capital Account.** In most business, a profit and loss statement is drawn up every month or so, showing how much profit (or loss) the business has experienced during the preceding period. (See Chapter 27). We know that profits represent increases in the proprietorship interest in the business. However, a good part of the periodic profits that are earned in a proprietorship will be withdrawn by the proprietor for his own personal use during the course of the year. This profit, therefore, doesn't represent a *permanent* increase in the capital account of the business and is usually *not* shown by increasing the capital account. Instead, this profit or loss is recorded in the temporary proprietorship account—the proprietor's drawing account. Profits are recorded by credits to the drawing account; losses are shown by debiting the drawing account.

Below we see the R. Robbins drawing account from the ledger. On March 2nd, March 9th, March 16th, March 23rd and March 30th, Mr. Robbins withdrew $100 for his own personal use. On March 31st, profit of $550 for the month was recorded in the account. Withdrawals are shown by debiting the account, and profits are recorded by credits to the account.

DATE		POST REF.	DEBIT	DATE		POST REF.	CREDIT
198– Mar 2		J4	100 00	198– Mar 31		J5	550 00
9		J4	100 00				
16		J4	100 00				
23		J5	100 00				
30		J5	100 00				

Robert Robbins Drawing   #302

Periodically, Mr. Robbins will review his drawing account. If he has credited more in profits to the account than he has withdrawn, he will have a credit balance in the account. At this point, he may decide to withdraw the credit balance in cash from the business. Or he may decide to leave these profits in the business permanently. In such a case, these profits be-

come a permanent part of the business' capital, and should be shown in the permanent capital account—Robert Robbins, capital, rather than in the temporary drawing account. The credit balance in the drawing account would then be closed out into the capital account, and the capital account would show a permanently larger balance. (See Chapter 29).

Returns and Allowances | 19

SALES RETURNS AND ALLOWANCES

Occasionally, a customer will return merchandise which he has bought previously. This is called a *sales return*. Or the customer may find that some of the merchandise he has bought is defective—perhaps broken in shipment, etc. When such a circumstance is called to the attention of the seller, he often grants the buyer a reduction in the total price without requiring the actual physical return of the merchandise. This is called a *sales allowance*.

CASH REBATES

If the merchandise was originally sold for cash, a *cash refund* or *rebate* will probably be granted. Most firms have a system whereby a cash rebate is authorized by a designated person who signs a cash refund slip for the customer. The customer then takes this to the cash register attendant or other qualified person and exchanges it for cash.

CREDIT MEMORANDUM

A special business form or document called a *credit memorandum* is used when a return or allowance is granted on merchandise originally *sold on account*. Credit memos vary in form with different firms, but they generally resemble the sales invoice that is prepared when goods are sold, except that the words "Credit Memorandum" appear on the top. Many firms use different colored papers for their credit memos and their sales invoices in order to avoid confusion. A credit memo usually includes date and name and address of seller and buyer. A space is provided for listing and describing the goods allowed for or returned, and the final amount of the return or allowance. Credit memos are numbered in consecutive order.

CREDIT MEMORANDUM

George Corp.
121 East 57 Street
New York, NY 10028

Date: March 15, 198__

In account with:

Joseph Smith
Avon Avenue   # 363
Spring Lake, NJ 07012

CREDIT:

5 flower pots @ $5 each	$25.00

In some firms, the signature of an authorized person is required on the face of all credit memoranda to make them valid.

JOURNALIZING RETURNS AND ALLOWANCES

When a return or allowance occurs, an asset account—either the cash or an account receivable—is decreased. This will be shown by crediting either cash or accounts receivable. The return of merchandise also means that sales have also been decreased. We could show this decrease in sales by directly debiting the sales account, but this is not usually done. Instead, a special account, *sales returns and allowances*, is debited. By use of this separate account, management is able to keep a separate record of all returns and allowances, rather than having them included as part of the sales account.

1. Cash Returns. When goods are returned for cash, *the sales returns and allowances account is debited and cash account is credited.* Here we see an example of a 4-column journal, showing an entry on April 5th of a $50 return of merchandise for cash. Similar entries would be made if the firm were using a combination journal or a cash receipts book.

						GENERAL	
CASH		DATE	NAME OF ACCOUNT	POST REF			
DEBIT	CREDIT				DEBIT	CREDIT	
	50 00	Apr. 5	Sales Returns & Allow.	450	50 00		

General Journal   Page 12

(19—)

2. Returns and Allowances of Merchandise Sold on Account. If customers return goods which were originally bought on *credit*, they will not receive cash, but the amount of money they owe the firm will be reduced. The bookkeeper receives notification of this in the form of a duplicate of the credit memo issued to the customer. The bookkeeper journalizes the returns or allowances of goods sold for credit by crediting the customer's account receivable and debiting sales return and allowance account.

There are various ways of recording these entries in a book of original entry, depending on the particular journal system used by the firm. A few methods are illustrated below, showing the journalizing of a return of $100 of merchandise by G. Carlin for credit to the Jones Hat Company. In every case the student should keep this general principle in mind—the customer's account must be credited, and the sales returns and allowances account must be debited.

a. GENERAL JOURNAL. The illustration below shows how the return might be entered in a 2-column general journal.

General Journal   Page 12

DATE	ACCOUNT TITLE	POST REF	DEBIT	CREDIT
(19—) Aug. 14	Sales Returns & Allowances	/	100 00	
	Accts'. Receivable, G. Carlin	/		100 00

At the time the transaction is journalized, a diagonal line is placed in the post. ref. column on the same line with the accounts receivable, G. Carlin entry.

When the entries are posted:

(1) The sales return and allowance ledger is *debited* with $100 and the number of the sales return and allowance account, #450, is written in the post. ref. column of the journal.

(2) The accounts receivable controlling account in the ledger is credited with $100, and the number of this account (120) is written above the diagonal line in the post. ref. column of the journal.

(3) The amount is also posted as a *credit* to the *individual customer's* account in the *accounts receivable ledger,* and a *check mark* is placed below the diagonal line in the journal.

Sales Returns and Allowances   Acct. #450

DATE	ITEM	POST REF	DEBIT	DATE	ITEM	POST REF	CREDIT
(19—) Apr. 14		J12	100 00				

Posting to the sales returns and allowance account.

Accounts Receivable   acct. #120

DATE	ITEM	POST REF	DEBIT	DATE	ITEM	POST REF	CREDIT
				198– Apr 14		J12	100 00

Posting to the accounts receivable controlling account.

G. Carlin
20 Hathaway Drive, City

DATE	ITEM	POST REF	DEBIT	CREDIT	DEBIT BALANCE
198– Apr 1		S2	500 00		500 00
14		J12		100 00	400 00

Posting to the individual customer's account in the accounts receivable ledger.

General Journal   Page 12

DATE	ACCOUNT TITLE	POST REF	DEBIT	CREDIT
198– Apr 14	Sales Returns and Allowances	450	100 00	
	Accts. Receivable, G. Carlin	120 ✓		100 00

The general journal after posting, showing entries in the post. ref. column.

b. COMBINATION JOURNAL. If a combination journal or a multi-columnar journal with special accounts receivable debit and credit columns is being used by the firm, a 2-line entry is required to journalize a sales return or allowance. On the first line, the date is entered, and the *sales return and allowance* is written in the *name of account column*. The amount is written in the *general debit column*. On the second line, the *customer's name* is written in the name of the account column, and the amount is written in the *accounts receivable credit column*.

Combination Journal   Page 19

| CASH | | DATE | NAME OF ACCOUNT | POST REF | GENERAL | | ACCTS. RECEIVABLE | |
DEBIT	CREDIT				DEBIT	CREDIT	DEBIT	CREDIT
		198– Apr 14	Sales Returns and Allow		100 00			
			G. Carlin					100 00

Posting these entries from the combination journal to the ledgers is done in the usual fashion. The $100 credit would be posted during the month to the G. Carlin account in the accounts receivable ledger and a check mark placed in the post. ref. column of the journal. The sales return and allowance debit of $100, which was entered in the general debit column, would be posted during the month to the sales return and allowance ledger account, and the number of that account (450) written in the journal post. ref. column. At the end of the month, the accounts receivable credit column would be totaled (as are all the other columns at the month's end) and the total in that column would be posted to the accounts receivable controlling account in the general ledger.

c. SALES RETURN AND ALLOWANCE JOURNAL. If a firm has a large number of sales returns and allowances, it may be useful to have a special *sales returns and allowances journal*, in which all returns or allowances *for credit* are entered. Each time the bookkeeper receives a duplicate of the credit memorandum, she journalizes this in the sales returns and allowances journal. Date, number of credit memo and customer's name are written on one line of the journal, and the amount is entered in the column provided.

| | DATE | | CREDIT MEMO | ACCOUNT | POST REF | ACCTS RECEIVABLE | | | CREDIT | | |
						SALES RET and ALLOW.			DEBIT		
	Sales Returns and Allowances Journal								*Page 49*		
1	198— Apr	6	3363	R. Harris	✓				5	0	00
2		14	3364	G. Carlin	✓				1 0	0	00
3		30	3365	A. Brown	✓				2	5	00
4		31							1 7	5	00
5									(450)	(120)	

This journal is posted at regular intervals *to the individual customer accounts* by crediting their accounts in the accounts receivable ledger. A check is placed in the post. ref. column of the sales returns and allowances journal to show that posting to the customer's account has been completed.

At the end of the month, the journal is totaled, and a double line drawn. The *total* is posted by *debiting the general ledger sales return and allowance account*, and *by crediting the accounts receivable controlling account* in the general ledger. The numbers of these accounts are written in parentheses under the double line in the amount column to show that posting has been completed.

PURCHASE RETURNS AND ALLOWANCES

Purchase returns and allowances occur when the firm *itself* buys merchandise from its suppliers and either returns it or receives an allowance.

If the merchandise was bought on credit, the firm will receive a credit memorandum from its supplier, showing the amount of the return or allowance. This credit memorandum is sent to the bookkeeper, and is used as the business document from which the journal entry to record the transaction is made.

As a result of the return or allowance, the amount of money that the firm owes its supplier will be reduced. The journal entries must show this reduction in accounts payable. This will be done by *debiting the creditor's account. Purchase returns and allowance account will be credited.*

The use of various different kinds of journals to record purchase returns and allowances is illustrated below. In each case, the journal records the fact that Jones Company has returned $25 of merchandise it had previously bought on account to the Goldfield Corp, and has received a credit memo from Goldfield to this effect.

1. **General Journal.**

	DATE		ACCOUNT	POST REF.	DEBIT		CREDIT	
	General Journal				*Page 12*			
	198— May	15	Accts Payable, Goldfield Corp		2 5	00		
			Purch. Ret. and Allow.				2 5	00

If the return is posted in a general journal, the student should remember that the debit must be posted to the accounts payable controlling account in the general ledger and also *to the individual creditor's account in the accounts payable ledger.* A line is drawn in the post. ref. column of the general journal when this debit is originally journalized, to remind the bookkeeper to post *to both accounts.* A check is placed in one half of the post. ref. column when the amount is posted to the Goldfield account in the accounts payable ledger, and the number of the accounts payable controlling account in the general ledger is written in the other half when the amount is debited to that account. Of course, posting will also involve posting the credit to the purchase return and allowance account in the general ledger.

2. **Combination Ledger.** If a combination journal or other multi-columnar journal with special accounts payable debit and credit columns is used, two lines are required to journalize a purchase return or allowance. The *name of the creditor* is written on the first line, and the amount is entered in the *accounts payable debit* column. *Purchase return and allowance* is written in the account column on the second line, and the amount is entered in the *general credit* column. Posting follows usual procedures.

| CASH | | | | | POST | GENERAL | | ACCOUNTS PAYABLE | |
DEBIT	CREDIT	DATE	ACCOUNT		REF	DEBIT	CREDIT	DEBIT	CREDIT
		199– May 19	Goldfield Corp.					25 00	
			Purch. Ret. and Allow.				25 00		

3. **Purchase Return and Allowance Journal.** Occasionally, a firm may have enough purchase returns or allowances to justify use of a special journal to record them.

Purchase Return and Allowance Journal				Page 7	
			POST	ACCTS' PAYABLE DEBIT	
DATE		NAME OF CREDITORS' ACCOUNT	REF	PURCH. RET. & ALLOW. CREDIT	
199– May 19		Goldfield Corp.		25 00	
	25	James Corp.		30 00	

NOTE: If a purchase return or allowance is made for *cash*, the transaction would result in an increase in cash, so the bookkeeper would debit cash and credit purchase return and allowance account. This could be journalized in a general 2- or 4-column journal, in a combination journal, or in the cash receipts journal.

TEST YOURSELF

Chapter 19

Identify or Explain.

1. Credit memorandum.
2. Sales allowance.
3. Sales returns and allowance account.
4. Purchase returns and allowance journal.

For each of the following transactions, state the accounts in the Ski Shop Company ledger which should be debited and credited:

1. A customer returns a pair of skis to Ski Shop for $25. He paid cash originally and receives cash.
2. Michael James returns a sweater to Ski Shop. He had originally charged the sweater to his account.
3. Ski Shop complains to its supplier, the Happy Boot Company, that 3 pairs of boots were received in unsalable condition. Happy Boot grants Ski Shop an allowance of $60.
4. Ski Shop returns two jackets to Green Jacket Company for credit.
5. Sandra Smith returns a hat previously bought and charged to her account.

Discounts on Purchases or Sales 20

TRADE DISCOUNTS

In many industries, manufacturers or wholesalers make it a practice to supply retailers with catalogues describing their products and listing the prices at which the merchandise might be resold to the retailers' customers. These prices are called *list prices*. The retailer obviously will pay the manufacturer less than the list price—and the price he pays is determined through a system of *trade discounts*. For example, Grey Kitchen Company may receive a catalogue from the Jones Plumbing Supply Company showing a kitchen sink listed at $100. Grey receives a trade discount of 40% from Jones Plumbing. Therefore, Grey's cost for the kitchen sink would be $100 less 40%, or $60.

When a system of trade discounts is used, merchandise is billed on the invoice and recorded in the books at the actual price charged, that is, the price *after* taking the trade discount. (In the above example, Grey would be billed for the sink at $60.) Therefore, *there is no need to make any special bookkeeping entries to reflect the trade discount.*

CASH DISCOUNT

A cash discount, however, is another matter. When a cash discount is permitted, the amount shown on the invoice and on the books does *not* reflect the cash discount, and special bookkeeping entries will be required to reflect the discount price.

1. **Explanation of Cash Discount.** In many industries, when goods are bought for credit, the seller will permit the buyer to pay a slightly smaller amount than the original bill if he pays the bill promptly within a certain stated period, rather than taking the full amount of time allowed before payment is actually due. This discount for extra-prompt payment is called a *cash discount*. (Cash discount is allowed only on value of merchandise and not on freight or other extra charges.)

2. **Terms on Which Most Credit Sales Are Made.** When a firm sells goods or services on credit to a customer, the *terms of sale* are stated on the invoice or bill. The buyer is told that he has a certain period of time by the end of which he must pay his bill in full. In addition, in those companies which allow a cash discount, the customer is told that if he pays his bill in advance, within a prescribed *shorter period*, he may deduct a certain percentage from the face amount of the bill—the cash discount.

3. **Statement of Terms of Sale.** This information about terms of sale is expressed in a kind of business shorthand:

   2/10 n/30 (read: two, ten—net, thirty)

This means that the entire bill is due for payment in *thirty* days, but the buyer may deduct 2% from the amount of the bill if he pays within *10* days of the date of the bill.

3/20 n/60 would mean that the entire bill is due in 60 days, but that a 3% discount may be taken if the bill is paid within 20 days of the date of the invoice.

The abbreviation EOM, for *end of month*, is also used in connection with terms of sale. 1/10 n/30 EOM means that the entire bill must be paid within 30 days *after the end of the month in which the invoice is dated*, but that a 1% discount may be taken if the bill is paid within 10 days *after the end of the month in which the invoice is dated*. For example, $1000 worth of merchandise is received by the Green Candy Company with an invoice dated May 20th. Terms of sale are 2/10 n/30 EOM. If Green pays the bill by June 10th (10 days after the end of the month in which the invoice is dated), they may deduct 2% or $20. Or else they may wait until June 30th (30 days after end of month in which invoice is dated) and pay the full face amount of the bill—$1000.

PURCHASE DISCOUNTS

Purchase discounts are the cash discounts taken by a business when it pays its bills promptly as stated in the terms of sale offered by a supplier.

1. **Analyzing Purchase Discounts.** When a firm pays its bills and takes advantage of a cash dis-

count, it pays its creditor less than the original amount of the bill. Nevertheless, the entire amount of the firm's indebtedness to the supplier is considered to have been paid, and the books must reflect this.

This situation is handled by debiting the creditor's account in the accounts payable ledger with the *full amount of the original bill*, regardless of the fact that a smaller amount has actually been paid. The cash account is credited with the actual amount of cash paid. The difference between the original bill and the amount of cash paid is the amount of the cash discount. This is credited to a general ledger account called *discount on purchases*.

For example, Brown Company receives an invoice from the Green Manufacturing Corp. for $1000, 2/10 n/60. This bill would be journalized and eventually posted to Green's account in the accounts payable ledger.

Green Mfg. Co.								
2700 Maple St., City								
DATE	ITEM	POST REF.	DEBIT		CREDIT		CREDIT BALANCE	
19__ Feb 3		P110			1000 00		1000 00	

Brown pays the bill within 10 days, sending Green a check for $980. Green's account must be *debited* with the full amount of the bill—$1000. Cash account must be *credited* with the amount of the payment—$980. Discount on purchases account must be *credited* with the amount of the cash discount—$20.

Thus, the two credit items (cash—$980 and discount on purchases—$20) equal the debit item (Green Company accounts payable—$1000).

This general procedure will be followed regardless of which journal a firm uses to record purchase discounts.

2. **Journalizing Purchase Discounts.** Purchase discounts can be journalized in several different journals, depending on the particular system of journals used by a company. Several examples are given below. In each case, the journal records the payment of $980 to Green Company analyzed above (original invoice—$1000, cash discount, $20).

a. GENERAL JOURNAL. Journalizing this transaction in a simple 2-column general journal involves a compound entry. On the first line, the debit of $1000 to accounts payable Green Co. is entered. On the next two lines, the two credit items—$20 to discount on purchases and $980 to cash—are entered.

General Journal				*Page 7*		
DATE	ACCOUNT	POST REF.	DEBIT		CREDIT	
19__ Feb 12	Accts. Payable — Green Corp.		1000 00			
	Discounts on Purchases				20 00	
	Cash				980 00	

b. COMBINATION JOURNAL. Many combination journals provide a special column for recording purchase discounts. When a firm uses such a combination journal, the name of the creditor is written in the name of account column, original amount of invoice ($1000) is entered in the *accounts payable debit* column, amount of cash payment

($980) is entered in the *cash credit column*, and the amount of the purchase discount ($20) is entered in the *purchase discount credit* column. (Note that the total amount of credits equals the total amount of debits.)

In posting these entries, the bookkeeper would post the $1000 debit to the Green Corp. account in the accounts payable ledger.

(A check would be placed in the post. ref. column to show that the entry had been posted to the individual creditor's account in the accounts payable ledger.) At the end of the month, the totals of the cash credit, purchase discount credit, accounts payable debit, etc., columns would be posted to their appropriate accounts in the general ledger.

| CASH | | | CHECK | | POST | GENERAL | | ACCOUNTS PAYABLE | | PURCHASE |
DEBIT	CREDIT	DATE	NO.	NAME OF ACCOUNT	REF.	DEBIT	CREDIT	DEBIT	CREDIT	DISCOUNT CREDIT
	980 00	Feb. 12	427	Green Corp.				1000 00		20 00

A Section of a Combination Journal, Showing Entry for a Payment where a Cash Discount was taken

c. CASH PAYMENTS JOURNAL. It is also possible to journalize payments involving purchase discounts directly in the cash payments journal. This is done by adding a special column, purchase discount credit, to the cash payments journal.

To record the payment of Green's invoice, follow the usual procedure for entering cash payments in the cash payments journal. Enter date, check number and name of creditor. Write the full amount of the invoice ($1000) in the accounts payable debit column. Write the amount of the cash payment ($980) in the cash credit column, and the amount of the purchase discount ($20) in the purchase discount credit column. Note that debit entries equal credit entries.

Cash Payments Journal Page 97

DATE	CHECK NO.	ACCOUNT DEBITED	POST REF.	GENERAL DEBIT	ACCT. PAY. DEBIT	CASH CREDIT	PURCHASE DISCOUNT CREDIT
Feb. 12	427	Green Corp.			1000 00	980 00	20 00

To post from the cash payments journal, follow the procedure outlined in Chapter 16 (Cash Payments Journal).

a. Post the $1000 debit directly to Green account in the accounts payable ledger.

b. At the month's end, post the total in accounts payable debit column, cash credit column and purchase discount credit column to the appropriate general ledger accounts.

SALES DISCOUNTS

We have seen above how a firm records the discounts on *purchases* which it *takes* on goods it purchases. We will now see how bookkeeping entries are made by a firm for discounts which it grants its *customers* on merchandise they buy. Such discounts are called *discounts on sales*, and they are granted to customers who pay their bills within a certain period of time, as stated in the terms of sale.

1. **Analyzing Discounts on Sales.** A company that allows its customers cash discounts for prompt payment must record these discounts in its books. For example, Adams Felt Company sells $100 of felt to the Better Hat Company, terms 2/10 n/30. Better Hat Company pays its bill within 10 days from date of invoice, sending Adams a check for $98 in full payment.

On its books, Adams must show: that Better Hat has paid its bill in full; that $98 in cash was received; that $2 of sales discounts were allowed.

This is done by crediting Better Hat Company account in accounts receivable ledger with $100; debiting cash account with $98;

debiting a general ledger account—*sales discounts*—with $2.

Note that total of debit entries equals total of credit entries.

2. **Journalizing Sales Discounts.** Journal entries for recording a cash receipt involving a sales discount depend on the journal system used by the firm. A few examples are given below, showing entries involved in recording the receipt of a check by Adams for $98 from Better Hat Company. The original invoice was for $100, and $2 cash discount was taken by Better Hat.

a. GENERAL JOURNAL. If the transaction is recorded in the general journal, a compound entry is required. Two debit items—a $98 debit to cash and a $2 debit to sales discount—are entered, and an offsetting $100 credit to accounts payable, Better Hat Company.

	General Journal		Page 21	

DATE	ITEM	POST REF	DEBIT	CREDIT
19-- Aug. 27	Cash		98 00	
	Sales discounts		2 00	
	Acct's. Payable, Better Hat			100 00

b. COMBINATION JOURNAL. Some firms provide a special column in the combination journal for recording sales discounts. In such a situation, the customer's name is written in the account column, $98 is written in the cash debit column, $2 is written in the sales discount debit column, and $100 is written in the accounts payable credit column.

CASH		DATE	ITEM	POST REF	GENERAL		ACCTS RECEIVABLE		SALES DISCOUNT DEBIT	ACCOUNTS PAYABLE		PURCHASE DISCOUNT CREDIT
DEBIT	CREDIT				DEBIT	CREDIT	DEBIT	CREDIT		DEBIT	CREDIT	
98 00		19-- Aug. 27	Better Hat Co.					100 00	2 00			

A Section of a Combination Journal with a Special Sales Discount Column

Posting follows the usual procedure—the $100 is posted as a credit to the individual customer's account in the accounts receivable ledger, and, at the month's end, the totals of all the columns are posted to the appropriate general ledger accounts.

c. CASH RECEIPTS JOURNAL. Sales discounts may be journalized directly in the cash receipts journal by providing a special column—*sales discount debit*—in this journal. When such a column is provided, payments by customers who take a discount for cash are journalized directly in the cash receipts journal. The name of customer is written in the name of account column. The amount of cash received ($98) is written in the cash debit column. The amount of the sales discount ($2) is written in the sales discount debit column. The original amount of the invoice ($100) is written in the accounts receivable credit column. (Note that total debits equal total credits.)

		Cash Receipts Journal				Page 25	

DATE	ITEM	POST REF	CASH DEBIT	SALES DISC DEBIT	ACCT. REC. CREDIT	SALES CREDIT	GENERAL CREDIT
19-- Aug. 27	Better Hat		98 00	2 00	100 00		

To post, the individual customer's account in the accounts receivable ledger would be credited with $100. At the month's end, the totals in the other columns would be posted to the appropriate general ledger accounts.

71

True or False.
1. When a *trade* discount is granted a customer, it must be recorded in the discount on sales account.
2. Cash discounts are granted *only* on those sales where cash is paid at the time of the sale.
3. If terms of sale are 2/20 n/60, a 2% discount will be allowed if the bill is paid within 20 days of date of invoice.
4. Jones Company takes a 2% cash discount when it pays its $100 bill due Brown Mfg. Co., sending Brown a check for $98. Brown should record this payment by crediting Jones' account for $98.
5. On April 1st, Sam Smith should pay Jones Company his bill for $50, dated March 1st, terms of sale 2/10 n/30. Sam Smith should pay Jones Company $50 less 2% or $49.
6. Harris Hat Company receives an invoice from the Jones Company for $100, dated April 10th, terms 2/10 n/30 EOM. Harris Company pays this bill on April 19th. Harris should send Jones a check for $98.
7. Harris Company pays its bill to Jones Company, taking a 2% discount for cash. Original invoice was for $100 and Harris sends Jones $98. The Jones Company bookkeeper should credit Harris' account with $98.
8. Cash discounts taken by customers should be debited to the sales discount account.
9. Purchase discounts taken by a company should be credited by the bookkeeper to the purchase discount account.
10. When a customer takes a cash discount, the sales discount, plus the amount of the payment, should equal the original invoice amount.

In each of the following examples, state debits and credits resulting from the transaction:

1. A customer pays a bill for $100, taking a $2 cash discount.
2. A customer pays a bill for $100 and does not take a cash discount.
3. A company pays a $500 invoice to a creditor, taking a $5 cash discount.
4. A company pays a $500 bill to a creditor, taking no discount.

Notes Payable and Notes Receivable | 21

Only non-interest bearing notes are discussed in this chapter. A full study of interest and interest bearing notes is made in Chapter 22.

PROMISSORY NOTES

A promissory note is an unconditional promise, made in writing, signed by one party, promising to pay another party a certain sum of money, either on demand, or at a specified future date. There are several important things to keep in mind in connection with promissory notes.

1. **Signed Promise to Pay.** Unlike obligations arising out of ordinary purchases of goods for credit (accounts receivable), a promissory note is a *signed* promise to pay.

2. **Usually Payable at a Specific Date.** Most notes are payable at a specific future date, although some may be payable on demand; that is, at the request of the person to whom the promise to pay is made.

3. **Promissory Notes Are Usually Negotiable.** The person holding the note can sell the note to a third person before it is due. Thus, if the person holding the note needs money before the due date, he can obtain it by selling the note. In business language, a note which is salable or transferable is said to be *negotiable*.

The person who signs the note and promises to pay the money is called the maker. The payee is the person or firm to whom the note is payable.

NEW YORK _May 14, 198-_

$200.00

Thirty days AFTER DATE _I_ PROMISE TO PAY

TO ORDER OF _Green Lumber Company_

Two Hundred and 00/100 ——————————— DOLLARS

PAYABLE AT _First National Bank of New York_

DATE DUE _June 13, 198-_

Robert Brown

Promissory Note

The example of a promissory note given here shows that Robert Brown (the maker) has promised to pay $200 to the Green Lumber Company (the payee) 30 days after the date of the note (May 14th). The money will be due on June 13th.

ENDORSING A PROMISSORY NOTE

One of the main attractions of a promissory note is that it is negotiable; that is, it can be sold or transferred in advance of the due date if the payee needs money in advance. For example, if Green Lumber Company needs money before the due date (June 13th for the above note), it can negotiate—transfer or sell—the note to a third party, probably Green's bank.

In order to transfer the note to Green's bank, Green must write his signature on the back of the note. This is called *endorsing the note.*

1. **Endorsement in Blank.**—When only the payee's signature appears on the back of the note, this is called an endorsement in blank. Such an en-

dorsement makes the note payable to whomever holds it on the due date.

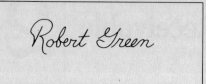

Endorsement in blank on back of note

2. **Endorsement in Full.** *An endorsement in full consists of payee's signature and instructions to pay the amount, when due, only to one certain specific party.* An endorsement in full offers protection in case the note is lost. It cannot be collected by anyone who finds it, since the instructions in the endorsement say that *only the person whose name is given in the endorsement may collect it.*

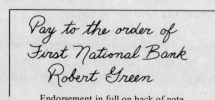

Endorsement in full on back of note

NOTES RECEIVABLE

1. **Origin of Notes Receivable.** A businessman may receive a note from a customer when a sale is made. This is *not* the usual procedure for selling goods on credit. (Usually credit is granted through accounts receivable, and no signed document is required.) However, sometimes customers with poor credit ratings may be required to sign such a note in order to get credit, because a signed note provides a stronger legal claim that an ordinary accounts receivable claim, should court action be required later on to force payment.

In other cases, a customer may have been granted credit through the ordinary accounts receivable channels at the time the sale was originally made. However, he may be unable to pay his bill when it comes due. At this point, the seller may request that the customer sign a note promising in *writing* to pay his debt at the end of a stated period of time.

These signed promises to pay represent monies owed *to* the business. They are therefore *assets* of the business. They are called *notes receivable.*

2. **Journalizing Notes Receivable Transactions.**
   a. NOTE RECEIVABLE AT TIME OF SALE. Sometimes a customer gives the company a note at the time of sale. The company's asset account (notes receivable) is increased, and its sales account is increased. This will be journalized *by debiting the notes receivable account and crediting the sales account.*

   Below we see a journal entry recording the fact that a sale of $200 of merchandise was made to R. Brown, and a note for $200 received from him.

| CASH | | | | | POST | GENERAL | | ACCOUNTS REC. | |
DEBIT	CREDIT	DATE	ACCOUNT		REF	DEBIT	CREDIT	DEBIT	CREDIT
		Mar 2	Notes Receivable			200 00			
			Sales				200 00		

Journal — Page 22

An alternative procedure is sometimes followed: In some firms, two sets of entries are required when a note is received from a customer at the time of the sale. *First,* the sale is debited to the customer's account in the accounts receivable ledger. (This is done in spite of the fact that a note has been received at the time of the sale.) Then, in a *second* set of entries made at the same time, the customer's accounts receivable is credited, and notes receivable is debited. In this way, there is a complete record of all credit ever extended to a customer (either through accounts receivable or notes receivable) in the customer's account in the accounts receivable ledger. Below is an example of such a set of entries showing a sale of $200 of merchandise to R. Brown and receipt of a note from him.

CASH DEBIT	CASH CREDIT	DATE	ACCOUNT	POST REF	GENERAL DEBIT	GENERAL CREDIT	ACCOUNTS REC. DEBIT	ACCOUNTS REC. CREDIT
		19— Mar 2	Robert Brown				200 00	
		2	Sales			200 00		
		2	Notes Receivable		200 00			
		2	Robert Brown					200 00

Journal — Page 22

b. NOTE RECEIVED FROM CUSTOMER WHOSE ACCOUNT RECEIVABLE IS OVERDUE. Sometimes a customer gives the company a note when the customer is unable to pay his bill when it comes due. When the company receives the customer's note, it has, in effect, exchanged one asset (the customer's account receivable) for another asset (the customer's note receivable). This would be shown in the journal by *debiting notes receivable* and *crediting accounts receivable*.

In the example below, Jacob Lawrence has given the Green Lumber Company a note for $500, which Green requested since Mr. Lawrence was unable to pay his account when it was due. The receipt of this note from Jacob Lawrence would be journalized in Green's journal as follows:

Journal — Page 22

CASH DEBIT	CASH CREDIT	DATE	ACCOUNT	POST REF	GENERAL DEBIT	GENERAL CREDIT	ACCOUNTS REC. DEBIT	ACCOUNTS REC. CREDIT
		19— Apr 19	Notes Receivable		500 00			
			Jacob Lawrence					500 00

c. PAYMENT BY A CUSTOMER OF HIS NOTE. When the due date arrives, and a customer pays his note, the company's asset cash is increased, and its asset notes receivable is decreased. This is journalized by *debiting cash* and *crediting notes receivable*. Below we see the journal entries that would be made on May 19th when Jacob Lawrence paid his note.

Journal — Page 25

CASH DEBIT	CASH CREDIT	DATE	ACCOUNT	POST REF	GENERAL DEBIT	GENERAL CREDIT	ACCOUNTS REC. DEBIT	ACCOUNTS REC. CREDIT
500 00		19— May 19	Notes Receivable			500 00		

3. Notes Receivable and the Balance Sheet. Notes receivable are listed as a current asset on the balance sheet, usually below accounts receivable.

NOTES PAYABLE

If a company *itself* signs a note payable to some individual firm, this note represents a debt or *liability* of the company, and is called *notes payable*.

1. Origin of Notes Payable. Notes payable often arise because a company can't pay its accounts payable on time, and the creditor requires a signed note. More commonly, notes payable arise in connection with borrowing monies from a bank. The usual procedure when a business borrows from a bank is for the bank to require a signed promissory note.

2. Journalizing Notes Payable.

a. NOTES ISSUED TO TRADE CREDITORS. (The term "trade creditors" refers to creditors to whom the firm owes debts arising out of normal business transactions, such as purchase of merchandise. The term is used to distinguish this kind of creditors from banks, etc., to whom the firm owes money.)

When a company is unable to pay its bills, the creditor may require a signed note payable. As a result of this, the company's former liability, accounts payable, is decreased. A new liability, notes payable, is increased. This is journalized by *debiting the creditor's account* in the accounts payable ledger, and *crediting the notes payable account.*

In the following example, Sanford Sweet Shop was unable to pay its bill for $600, due April 24th, to Crumb Candy. Crumb Candy requested a signed 30-day note from Sanford Sweet Shop. This was recorded in the Sanford journal as follows:

CASH					POST	GENERAL		ACCOUNTS REC.		ACCOUNTS PAY
DEBIT	CREDIT	DATE	ACCOUNT		REF.	DEBIT	CREDIT	DEBIT	CREDIT	DEBIT	C
		Apr 24	Crumb Candy							600 00	
			Notes Payable				600 00				

Combination Journal — Page 33

b. NOTES ISSUED TO BANK. When a company borrows money from a bank, an asset account (cash) is increased, and a liability account (notes payable) is increased. This is journalized by *debiting cash* and *crediting notes payable.* This could be journalized in the combination journal shown above (write notes payable in account column, enter the debit in the cash debit column, and the credit in the general credit column) or in a cash receipts journal. Here we see entries in the cash receipts journal, showing a note issued to the bank for $1000.

Cash Receipts Journal — Page 37

| DATE | ACCOUNT CREDITED | POST REF. | GENERAL CREDIT | SALES CREDIT | ACCT. REC CREDIT | DISC. ON SALES DEBIT | CASH DEBIT |
| Sept 12 | Notes Payable – Bank | | 1000 00 | | | | 1000 00 |

c. ENTRIES WHEN A NOTE IS PAID. When the company pays off a note payable, an asset account (cash) is decreased, and a liability account (notes payable) is decreased. This is journalized by *debiting notes payable* and *crediting the cash account.* Depending on the journal system used by the firm, entries could be made in the combination journal or the cash payments journal. Here we see entries to record payment by Sanford Sweet Shop of its note payable to Crumb Candy on May 24th.

Combination Journal — Page 34

CASH					POST	GENERAL		ACCOUNTS REC.		ACCOUNTS PAY
DEBIT	CREDIT	DATE	ACCOUNT		REF.	DEBIT	CREDIT	DEBIT	CREDIT	DEBIT	CREDIT
	600 00	May 24	Notes Payable – Crumb Candy			600 00					

Cash Payments Journal — Page 14

| DATE | CHECK NO. | ACCOUNT DEBITED | POST REF. | GENERAL DEBIT | ACCTS PAY DEBIT | CASH CREDIT |
| May 24 | 123 | Notes Payable – Crumb Candy | | 600 00 | | 600 00 |

d. NOTES PAYABLE ON THE BALANCE SHEET. Notes payable are listed as a current liability on the balance sheet, usually following accounts payable.

Chapter 21

Identify or Explain.
1. Promissory note.
2. *Maker* of a promissory note.
3. Negotiable promissory note.
4. Endorsing a promissory note.
5. Notes payable.
6. Notes receivable.

For each of the following transactions, state the accounts in the Blue Manufacturing Company ledger which should be debited and which should be credited:

1. Blue Mfg. obtains a note from Cynthia Hardware Company when Cynthia is unable to pay its account.
2. Cynthia Hardware pays off the note when it is due.
3. Blue Manufacutring borrows from Central City Bank, signing a note.
4. Blue Manufacturing is unable to pay its bill to U.S. Steel Company—and at U.S. Steel's request, gives U.S. Steel its note promising to pay the account within 60 days.
5. Blue Mfg. pays its note to U.S. Steel when it becomes due.

Below is an empty sheet from the Adams Company combination journal. The following transactions took place during April. Enter them in the Adams Company journal.

April 1. Arthur Jay returned $100 of merchandise previously bought on credit.
April 2. Richard Smith returned $50 of merchandise bought for cash. He was given cash for the merchandise.
April 3. Adams Company received an allowance of $20 from Harris Supply for defective merchandise previously shipped.
April 6. Adams Company paid a $1000 bill owed to Harris, deducting a $20 cash discount.
April 7. Richard Smith paid Adams his bill for $200, deducting a $4 cash discount.
April 8. Arthur Jay paid Adams $50 on account.
April 9. Jim Green returned $40 worth of merchandise previously bought on credit.
April 10. Adams gave First National Bank a note for $1000 and received cash.
April 13. Gladys Smith could not pay her account and gave Adams her note for $75.
April 15. Sam Richards paid off his note for $100 which he had previously given to Adams.
April 16. Adams paid off a $500 note previously written to Gold Engraving Corp.
April 19. Adams bought $1000 of merchandise on credit from Soap Superior Corp.

Combination Journal

DATE	ITEM	POST REF	CASH DEBIT	CREDIT	GENERAL DEBIT	CREDIT	ACCTS. RECEIV. DEBIT	CREDIT	SALES DISCOUNT DEBIT	ACCOUNTS PAYABLE DEBIT	CREDIT	PURCHASE DISCOUNT CREDIT

Interest and Interest-Bearing Notes | 22

INTEREST-BEARING NOTES

We saw in Chapter 21 how promissory notes are used in business. Some promissory notes require that the signer pay interest on the amount of the note. Such notes are called *interest-bearing notes*. Notes that do *not* require the payment of interest are called *non-interest-bearing notes*. Interest is the charge or cost paid for using money or credit.

COMPUTING INTEREST

The interest on an interest-bearing note is stated in terms of a percentage, for example 8%. This means that the interest charge will be 8 cents a year for *each* dollar borrowed for *one* year. To determine the amount of interest in *dollars* on a particular note, we must know the interest rate, the period of time, and the number of dollars involved.

1. **Interest Rate.** The interest rate is expressed as a percentage, $7\frac{1}{2}\%$, etc.
2. **Period of Time.** The period of time for which the money or credit is advanced is stated in the note. To compute interest, state the period of time as a *fraction of a year*. For example, a six-month note is said to involve $\frac{1}{2}$ a year, and a three-month note involves $\frac{3}{12}$ or $\frac{1}{4}$ of a year. In computing interest, a year is usually assumed to be 360 days, and each month is assumed to have 30 days. Money borrowed for 30 days is said to be borrowed for $\frac{1}{12}$ of a year ($\frac{30}{360}$); money borrowed for 60 days is said to be borrowed for $\frac{2}{12}$ of a year, etc.
3. **Principal.** The principal is the amount of money or credit advanced. The formula for computing interest is Principal $\times$ rate $\times$ time = dollar amount of interest. To figure the interest on a four-month note for $1000 at 8%,

multiply $1000 times $\frac{8}{100}$ times $\frac{4}{12}$ ($1000 $\times$ $\frac{8}{100}$ $\times$ $\frac{4}{12}$ = $26.67). To compute interest on a 30-day note for $2000 at 10%, the following computation would be done:

$$\$2000 \times \tfrac{10}{100} \times \tfrac{1}{12} = \$16.67$$

(Note that $\frac{1}{12}$ was used for the period of time, since 30 days is considered one-twelfth of a 360-day year.)

RECORDING INTEREST COST

When a firm signs an interest-bearing note, the interest must be paid at the time the note is due and paid. The interest is an expense of the business. When the interest is paid, the cash account is decreased, so *cash is credited*, and the *interest expense account is debited*.

1. **Analyzing a Transaction Involving Interest Expense.** Hawkins company has signed a note for $1000 at 10% for six months. At the end of the six months, Hawkins must pay the holder of the note $1000 plus $50 of interest, or $1050. Hawkins' books must show: cash decreased by the amount of the payment ($1050); notes payable decreased by amount of the note ($1000) that has been paid; and interest expense of $50 incurred. This is done by crediting cash $1050, debiting notes payable $1000, and debiting interest expense $50.
2. **Journalizing a Transaction Involving Interest Expense.** Payment of an interest-bearing note can be journalized in the *cash payments* journal. The transaction will require *two* lines in the journal since there are *two* accounts (notes payable and interest expense) to be *debited*.

Cash Payments Journal   Page 17

DATE	CHECK NO.	ACCOUNT DEBITED	POST REF.	GENERAL DEBIT	ACCTS. PAY DEBIT	CASH CREDIT
198- May 15	395	Notes Payable		1000 00		1050 00
		Interest Expense		50 00		

RECORDING INTEREST INCOME

A firm will receive interest in connection with the payment of an interest-bearing *note receivable* which it holds. This interest is additional income to the firm. This interest income is recorded in a ledger account *called interest income* account. When the interest is received, cash is increased, so the *cash account is debited. The interest income account is credited.*

1. **Analyzing a Transaction Involving Interest Income.** Harry Hennessey has given the Rich Manufacturing Company his 8% note for $1000, due in 60 days. At the end of 60 days, Mr. Hennessey pays the note ($1000) and the interest due ($13.33).

Rich Manufacturing journal must show that:

a. Rich Manufacturing cash has increased by the amount of Mr. Hennessey's payment ($1013.33).
b. Rich Manufacturing notes receivable account has been decreased by $1000.
c. Rich has received interest income of $13.33.

This is done by debiting cash $1013.33; crediting notes receivable $1000; and crediting interest income $13.33.

2. **Journalizing Transactions Involving Interest Income.** The receipt of interest income involves a receipt of cash, so the transaction can be journalized in the cash receipts journal. Two lines will be required to journalize the receipt of interest in connection with repayment of a note, since two accounts (notes receivable and interest income) must be credited.

Cash Receipts Journal   Page 17

DATE	ACCOUNT CREDITED	POST REF	GENERAL CREDIT	SALES CREDIT	ACCT. REC. CREDIT	DISC. ON SALES DEBIT	CASH DEBIT
19— Sept 5	Notes Receivable		1000 00				1013 33
	Interest Income		13 33				

If the firm did not keep a special cash receipts journal, it would be possible to journalize the transaction in the combination journal. In such a case, two lines would be required to list the two general credit items (notes receivable and interest income).

Combination Journal   Page 23

CASH DEBIT	CREDIT	DATE	ACCOUNT	POST REF	GENERAL DEBIT	GENERAL CREDIT	ACCTS. REC. DEBIT	ACCTS. REC. CREDIT	ACCTS. PAY. DEBIT	ACCTS. PAY. CREDIT
1013 33		19— Sept 5	Notes Receivable			1000 00				
			Interest Income			13 33				

Chapter 22

For each of the following transactions, list the debits and credits required to record the transaction in the Ferry Company Journal.

1. Ferry Company sells Robert Brown merchandise and receives a 90-day 10% interest-bearing note for $1000 from him.
2. Robert Brown pays off his note by giving Ferry Company $1025.
3. Ferry Company receives a $500 60-day non-interest-bearing note from Sam Jones when Sam Jones is unable to pay his account on time.
4. Sam Jones pays his $500 note when due.
5. Ferry Company pays off a 8% 6-month note for $2000 due the Smith Manufacturing Company and sends Smith a check for $2080.
6. Ferry Company pays off a 3-month non-interest-bearing note for $500 due Sanders Company.
7. Ferry Company receives a check for $1030 from James Harvey in payment of a 4-month 9% note for $1000 he had signed four months earlier.

Banking Procedures 23

USE OF CHECKING ACCOUNT

Most business payments are made by check, and most businesses have *checking accounts* at a local commercial bank. The use of a checking account rather than cash is desirable for several reasons. Cash can be lost or stolen. A checking account makes it possible to pay bills without keeping large amounts of cash on hand. A cancelled check is a permanent record of payment and provides legal evidence that payment has been made.

OPENING A CHECKING ACCOUNT

When a new account is opened at a bank, a *signature card* must be filled out and kept by the bank. *Each person who is authorized to sign checks for the company must sign the signature card.

MAKING A DEPOSIT

A bank deposit may consist of cash items (currency and coins) and non-cash items. Non-cash items include checks that the company has received from others, money orders, travellers' checks, etc.

1. **Endorsing Checks.** Each check that the company has received from others and is deposited must be "endorsed." This is done by writing the name of the depositor on the back of the check. The endorsement may be written by hand or rubber stamped. The preferred form of endorsement—endorsement in full—reads: "For deposit in First National Bank of Florida John T. Smith."

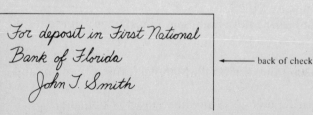

For deposit in First National Bank of Florida John T. Smith ← back of check

Endorsement in full.

There is also another form of endorsement, called "endorsement in blank." This consists only of the depositor's name. Endorsement in blank makes the check payable to the *bearer;* that is, to anyone who holds it. Therefore, if a check that is endorsed in blank is lost, it can be cashed by anybody who finds it. Endorsement in *full* makes the check payable *only* to the person or bank named in the endorsement, and as such, gives more protection in case the check is lost or stolen.

John T. Smith ← back of check

Endorsement in blank.

2. **Preparing a Deposit Slip.** Each time a bank deposit is made, a *deposit slip* listing all the items (cash, checks, etc.) must accompany it. The deposit slip is usually prepared in duplicate by the bookkeeper or cashier. The bookkeeper gives the two slips and the cash and checks to the teller at the bank, who keeps one of the deposit slips. The other is stamped by the teller and kept by the bookkeeper as a receipt for the deposit.

On the deposit slip, the bookkeeper lists the total amount of coins being deposited and total amount of bills (paper money). Then he lists each check individually. In some firms, checks are further indicated by writing the name of the person from whom the check was received, or the ABA number, which is printed on each check. Finally, any money orders, etc., to be deposited are listed.

```
FIRST NATIONAL BANK
    of FLORIDA
GAINSVILLE, FLORIDA


ACCOUNT    John T. Smith

           25 Lee Street

DATE       March 12, 198-


BILLS                      50  00
COIN                        1  25
CHECKS                    120  00
                           64  50
                           71  25


                          305  75
```

Bank Deposit Slip

the deposits and of all the withdrawals he has made (checks he has written). Thus he can tell at any time the amount of his bank balance.

WRITING A CHECK

When a depositor opens an account, the bank gives him a checkbook, consisting of checks and check stubs. When the depositor wishes to pay a bill, he writes a check, which, in effect, orders his bank to pay a stated amount of cash from his bank account to the person to whom the check is written. Checks are usually numbered—they may be prenumbered by the bank, or the depositor may number them in order as he writes them.

To write a check, fill in the date, the name of the payee (the person or company to whom the check is made payable) and the amount of the check. The amount is written out once in words, and once in numbers. When writing out the amount in words, be sure to start at the extreme left side of the space provided, so that no alterations may be made later on. Every check must be signed by a person authorized on the signature card filed with the bank.

3. Entering Deposits on the Check Stub. The check stub of the check book provides spaces for recording all deposits. The amount of each deposit as recorded on the deposit slip is recorded on the check stub, and the balance in the account brought up to date. By consulting his check book, a depositor has a record of all

THE CHECK STUB

It is very important to fill out the check stub at the time the check is originally written. The amount of the check is subtracted from the previous balance as recorded on the stub; any deposit made in the meantime is added, and a new balance is drawn. In many firms the purpose of the check is also recorded on the stub (i.e., for salaries, etc.).

```
NO. 56          FIRST NATIONAL BANK OF FLORIDA        63-202
                                                        751

DATE Mar. 25,198-   No. 56        GAINSVILLE.  March 25,198-

TO  Jones Mfg.    Pay to order of  Jones Manufacturing Corp.   $21 60/100

FOR Invoice of 3/12    Twenty one 60/100 _____ DOLLARS
BALANCE    550.00
DEPOSIT     72.50           Richard Smith
TOTAL      622.50
THIS CHECK  21.60
BALANCE    600.90
```

Check

81

BANK STATEMENT

At the end of the month the bank sends each depositor a bank statement.

1. **Description of Bank Statement.** The bank statement shows the balance (amount of money) in the depositor's account in the beginning of the month, all the deposits that have been made during the month, all the withdrawals (checks that have been written and cashed) during the month, service charges, etc., and the *balance* in the depositor's account *at the end of the month according to the bank's records.*

2. **Cancelled Checks.** A number of paid or cancelled checks is returned to the depositor with his bank statement. The *cancelled checks* are those that were written by the depositor *and cashed* (presented for payment to the bank) during the period covered by the statement.

3. **Service Charges.** Often the bank will make a charge to the depositor for extra services that have been performed during the month. Some banks also charge a monthly service charge when the average amount of money the depositor has in the bank during the month falls below a certain balance.

DIFFERENCES BETWEEN BANK STATEMENT BALANCE AND CHECKBOOK BALANCE

When the depositor receives his bank statement from the bank at the end of the month, the bank balance as shown by the bank usually does *not* agree with the balance as shown on his check stub. There are several reasons that may account for this difference.

1. **Unrecorded Deposits.** The depositor may have just mailed a deposit to his bank. The depositor has recorded this deposit on his check stub, but the deposit may not have reached the bank in time to be recorded on the bank statement.

2. **Outstanding Checks.** The depositor may have written checks to others and deducted the amount of these checks from his balance on his check stub. These checks, however, have not as yet been presented to the bank for payment. Therefore, the bank has no record of them, and has not deducted them from the depositor's balance. Checks that have been written but have not been presented for payment are called *outstanding checks.*

3. **Service Charges.** The bank may have made a service charge to the depositor and deducted this amount from the depositor's balance. Notification to the depositor may not have taken place as yet, however. Therefore, the depositor has not deducted the amount of the service charge from his bank balance as shown in his stubs, but the bank has deducted it from his balance as shown on the bank statement.

BANK RECONCILIATION

In order to make sure that both his records and the bank's records are accurate, the bookkeeper must attempt to bring the two into agreement by accounting for the differences. This is called *preparing a bank reconciliation,* or *reconciling the bank statement.* The following steps are taken to prepare a bank reconciliation.

1. Take all cancelled checks received from the bank and arrange them in order of check numbers.

2. Place a check mark on the appropriate check stub in the checkbook for each cancelled check.

3. Working from the unchecked check stubs, make a list of all checks which have been written but which have *not* been returned as cancelled checks. These are the *outstanding* checks.

4. Compare bank statement with check stubs. Make a list of any bank service charges listed on the bank statement for which no record has been made in the check stubs during the month.

5. Compare bank statement with check stubs. Make a list of any deposits listed on the check stubs which are not listed on the bank statement.

6. Draw up reconciliation. With all of the above information in hand, it is possible to draw up the bank reconciliation.

   a. On one side of a paper write the balance as of your check stub. *Deduct* any service charges reported in bank statement but not recorded to date in your check stubs. The resulting figure is *your corrected check stub balance.*

   b. On the other side of the paper, write the balance as reported on your bank statement. *List and deduct* all outstanding checks. *Add* any deposits recorded in your check stubs but not on the bank statement. The resulting figure is the *corrected bank statement balance.*

The two balances should be equal. If they are, the bank statement is said to be reconciled. If they are not, your check stubs should be checked for arithmetic mistakes, the bank's figures should be checked for arithmetic mistakes, and the entire procedure should be checked and repeated for omissions and/or errors.

NOTE

Service charges made by the bank must be recorded in the books of the company. They are charged to *miscellaneous expense account*. Journal entries are made to *debit miscellaneous expense* and *credit cash*. This can be done in the general or combination journal, or if the firm keeps a cash payments journal, it can be recorded there.

HORACE COMPANY
Bank Reconciliation, September 30, 198—

Balance on check stub Sept 30	$1050.31	Balance on bank statement Sept 30		$ 986.31
Deduct: Service charge	4.00	*Deduct:* Outstanding checks		
		Check # Amount		
		111 25.00		
		114 75.00		100.00
				886.31
		Add: Unrecorded deposit Sept 29		160.00
Correct Check Stub Balance	$1046.31	Correct Bank Balance		$1046.31

Chapter 23

Identify or Explain.

1. Bank signature card.
2. Endorsement in full.
3. Deposit slip.
4. Cancelled checks.
5. Outstanding checks.

Problem:

Robert Jones' checkbook shows a balance of $600. His bank statement shows a balance of $580. A study of his checkbook, cancelled checks and bank statement reveals that there is one check for $10 outstanding; and that a bank service charge of $5 has been charged on his statement but not recorded in his checkbook, also that a deposit of $25 was recorded in his checkbook but not on his bank statement. Prepare a bank reconciliation.

The Petty Cash System | 24

CASH TRANSACTIONS

In most businesses, all the cash that is received is deposited in the bank, and, as far as possible, all cash payments are made by check rather than with actual currency. This is done to provide a permanent record (in the form of bank statements and check stubs) of all monies coming in to the firm and of all monies going out. However, in any business, there will be some small expenses which must be paid in currency rather than by check. Such expenses will include postage due the postman on mail delivered, collect telegrams, carfare for an office boy sent on an errand, etc.

PETTY CASH SYSTEM

A special system must be set up by a business to control the small fund of currency which is kept on hand for such expenses. This fund is called the *petty cash fund* and the procedures governing its use are called the *petty cash system*. (The methods described here are for use of an *imprest* petty cash fund—the most widely used system.)

1. **General Principles in Handling Petty Cash**. Several principles should be kept in mind in connection with handling of petty cash.

   a. SEPARATE FUND. Petty cash should be kept separate from all other cash involved in the business. For example, it should *never* be intermingled with cash received in the course of business from customers.

   b. ONE PERSON RESPONSIBLE FOR PETTY CASH. Good business procedure makes one person responsible for handling petty cash, and all withdrawals from the petty cash must be made through this person.

2. **Establishing a Petty Cash Fund.** When a petty cash fund is first set up, a check is written for the amount required (perhaps $50). This check is made out to Petty Cash. The check is cashed, and the $50 in currency and coins are given to the person responsible for handling petty cash, and placed in a petty cash box or drawer.

   The journal entries made when the check is written should show that the regular cash account of the firm has been decreased and that a new asset ledger account—petty cash account—has been increased. This is done by *crediting cash account* and *debiting petty cash account*.

   These journal entries can be made in a general or combination journal if the firm uses one, or in the cash payments journal.

   Here we see how the entry for setting up a petty cash fund of $50 would be recorded in a general journal. Note that the petty cash account is debited and cash account is credited.

Here we see how the same transaction would be recorded in the cash payments journal.

When either of these journals is posted to the ledger, the regular cash account of the business is credited and a new ledger account—petty cash—is debited.

3. **Disbursements From Petty Cash Fund.** Everytime anybody in the firm requires money from the petty cash fund, he must fill out and sign a numbered *petty cash voucher*, showing date, amount and purpose of payment. In some firms, the signature of another person authorizing the payment must also appear. These petty cash vouchers are filed in the petty cash drawer or box after they are filled out.

```
┌─────────────────────────────────────────────┐
│ #25            Barbara Shoe Corp.            │
│                Petty Cash Voucher            │
├─────────────────────────────────────────────┤
│                                              │
│                    Date  Mar. 14, 198-       │
│                                              │
│                           ┌──────────────┐   │
│                           │    amount     │   │
│  Pay  Postman             │   $1.50       │   │
│                           └──────────────┘   │
│  For  Postage Due on Package                 │
│                                              │
│   J. Smith                  H. Brown         │
│   Payment Received          Authorized       │
└─────────────────────────────────────────────┘
```

4. **Proving or Checking Petty Cash.** We have seen how each disbursement (money paid out) from petty cash requires a petty cash voucher for the amount of the cash taken from the petty cash drawer. Therefore, at any time, the total of cash in the petty cash drawer, plus amount of vouchers, should always equal the original amount of cash in petty cash. In many firms, the petty cash is "proven" at intervals (perhaps every day) by adding cash on hand to amounts recorded on petty cash vouchers, and seeing if the total does equal the original amount of petty cash.

5. **Replenishing Petty Cash.** When the petty cash fund gets low, or at any event, at the end of the month, the petty cash fund must be replenished or brought back to its original level.

a. WRITING CHECK TO REPLENISH PETTY CASH FUND. The vouchers in the petty cash drawer are totaled, and a check equal to that total is written. The check is made out to petty cash.

EXAMPLE. On March 1st, a petty cash fund was established with $50. By March 31st, $45 of vouchers were on hand, $5 was left in the petty cash fund. A check for the amount of the vouchers ($45), made out to petty cash, was written and cashed, thus bringing the petty cash fund back to its original $50 level.

b. RECORDING THE CHECK THAT REPLENISHES PETTY CASH FUND. When the petty cash fund is replenished, the amount of the check constitutes a *decrease* in the regular cash account of the firm, so the cash account will be *credited*. The offsetting debit is determined by taking the petty cash vouchers, sorting them, and *debiting the accounts as indicated on the petty cash vouchers*.

EXAMPLE. We saw in the above example that $45 of petty cash vouchers had been written during March, and that a check for $45 was written on March 31st to replenish the petty cash fund. These vouchers are sorted, in accordance with the purpose of each payment. A summary of the vouchers shows that payments were made for the following purposes:

$10	Postage expense.
15	Delivery expense.
20	Miscellaneous expense.
$45	

Therefore, to record the check for $45 which has been written to replenish petty cash fund, the bookkeeper would credit the cash account, and debit $10 to postage expense account, $15 to the delivery expense account, and $20 to miscellaneous expense.

This could be recorded in a general journal or in the cash payments journal.

CASH		CHECK		ACCOUNT	POST	GENERAL	
DEBIT	CREDIT	NO.	DATE		REF.	DEBIT	CREDIT
	45 00	385	19— Mar. 31	Postage Expense		10 00	
				Delivery Expense		15 00	
				Miscellaneous Expense		20 00	

General Journal — Page 59

Note that *no further entries are made in the petty cash account once the petty cash fund has been opened.* Every time the petty cash account is replenished, *the offsetting debits are to the expense accounts* recorded on the petty cash vouchers from the previous period, and *not to petty cash account.*

SUMMARY

Businesses try to make most payments by check, but some currency payments are required and these are handled through a petty cash system. A petty cash fund is established by writing and cashing a check drawn to petty cash, and placing the currency in a special petty cash drawer or box. Each time money is taken out of the petty cash drawer, a petty cash voucher must be filled out. When the petty cash fund is established, the petty cash account is debited and the cash account is credited. Each month, the petty cash fund is replenished and brought back to its original level by writing and cashing a check for the total indicated on the vouchers written during the preceding month. This check is debited to the proper accounts in accordance with the vouchers written during the previous month, and is credited to cash.

TEST YOURSELF

Chapter 24

True or False.

1. Good business procedure involves making as many payments as possible by check rather than by cash.
2. Good business procedure encourages the intermingling of the petty cash fund with whatever cash is received from customers in the normal course of business.
3. To set up a petty cash fund, debit the petty cash account and credit the cash account.
4. The balance in the petty cash account that appears in the ledger should equal the amount of currency in the petty cash box, plus the amount of petty cash vouchers in the petty cash box.
5. A petty cash voucher is filled out only when the petty cash box is replenished with additional cash.
6. Both the check that sets up the petty cash fund originally and each check that is written to replenish the fund are debited to petty cash and credited to cash account.
7. When the petty cash fund is replenished, credit the cash account and debit the expense account as shown on the petty cash vouchers in the petty cash box.
8. The petty cash ledger account shows a balance of $50. There are $28 worth of petty cash vouchers in the petty cash box. For the petty cash to "prove," there should be $50 in currency in the petty cash box.
9. Good business practice requires that a petty cash voucher be completed each time any money is taken out of the petty cash box.
10. To prove petty cash, add cash on hand to amounts recorded on vouchers and see if that total equals the original amount of petty cash.
11. A typical use of petty cash is to pay bills for merchandise, furniture or equipment, and weekly payroll.

Payrolls and Payroll Taxes 25

PAYROLL

A payroll is a list of all the employees of a firm and the total amount of wages or salaries due them for a given period. Payrolls are prepared weekly, semi-monthly or monthly, depending on the firm. Before paying his workers, the employer must hold back or "withhold" certain payroll taxes from the wages due his employees. For each payday, the payroll clerk or bookkeeper prepares a list showing the gross amount each employee has earned, the amounts deducted from his gross salary (taxes withheld), and the net amount of salary which will be paid to him. This is called a *payroll register*.

PAYROLL TAXES

There are several kinds of payroll taxes which, *by law*, must be withheld by the employer from his workers' paychecks. The employer is required to withhold these taxes each payday, and then, at specified intervals (usually every month, but this varies) send these monies to the appropriate government agency. There are also certain taxes based on the amount of the payroll that must be paid only by the *employer*.

1. **Social Security Taxes.** Social security taxes include the FICA tax (Federal Insurance Contributions Act) which provides old-age benefits to workers who retire or are disabled. It also provides benefits to widows and dependents of dead or disabled workers. There are also various unemployment taxes which provide payment to those temporarily unemployed.

    The FICA tax is paid by *both* the employer and the employee. Congress has passed legislation providing for steadily increasing FICA rates for the late 1970's and early 1980's. For 1981 the rate of this tax is 6.65% of the first $29,700 earned in the year. This would mean that 6.65% of each employee's salary up to $29,700 a year must be withheld by the employer, and that another 6.65% of the first $29,700 must be set aside and paid by the employer. These monies are sent to the Internal

Revenue Service, and form the basis for the old age and disability insurance discussed above. (Note that if a worker earns more in one year than the maximum amount taxable for FICA purposes, neither he nor his employer pays *FICA* tax on the excess.)

    Other taxes are the federal and state unemployment taxes. These taxes are also based on payrolls, and consist of a stated percentage of each employee's wages, but they are generally paid only by the *employer* and are not withheld from employees' wages.

2. **Income Taxes.** The *federal government* requires that each employer withhold part of his employees' wages as a help in collecting the federal income tax. The amount to be withheld is determined by consulting a *withholding chart or table* prepared by the Internal Revenue Service. This tells how much should be withheld for income tax purposes in various salary ranges, depending on exemptions (i.e., number of dependents, marital status, etc.). From time to time Congress changes tax laws and rates and the Internal Revenue Service supplies new withholding tables.

    Certain states and cities (i.e. New York State and New York City) also require employers to withhold state and local income taxes from their employees' wages. The same principles apply as for federal income tax withholding.

RECORD KEEPING IN CONNECTION WITH PAYROLLS AND PAYROLL TAXES

By law the employer *is required* to withhold the above taxes from his employees' salaries. The law also requires that he keep his payroll records for four years, that he furnish the government at stated intervals with reports on and payments of taxes withheld, and that at the end of the year, he provide each employee with a statement of the employee's total wages for the year, and of the total of FICA and income tax withholdings. The *withholding statement* on which this information is supplied to each employee is called Form *W-2*, and can be obtained by the firm from the Internal Revenue Service. Every employee must file copies of all W-2 forms received, stapled to his income tax return for the year.

BOOKKEEPING ENTRIES FOR PAYROLLS AND EMPLOYERS' PAYROLL TAXES

The journal entries that are made when each payroll is prepared show the total amount of the payroll. This is usually recorded in the journal by charging (debiting) the amount to an expense account called *salary expense*. The journal must also show that some of this salary expense was actually paid out in cash to the employees, but that some was withheld by the employer as FICA and income tax withholdings. This is done by:

1. Debiting salary expense for the total amount of the payroll;
2. Crediting cash for the actual amount of cash paid to employees;
3. Crediting the FICA tax payable account and employees' federal income tax payable account for the amounts withheld.

For example, assume the total payroll of the Brown Manufacturing Company is $500.00 as shown in the following payroll register:

Payroll Register

NAME	TOTAL EARNINGS	F.I.C.A. TAX	INCOME TAX	OTHER DEDUCTIONS	NET PAY	CHECK NO.
Week Ended March 7				Date of Payment March 7		
Mary Green	300 00	19 95	60 00		220 05	157
John Wong	200 00	13 30	30 00		156 70	158
	500 00	33 25	90 00		376 75	

Journal entries must show that $500 salary expenses was incurred (*debit salary expense $500*); that cash of $376.75 was paid out (*credit cash $376.75*) and that the company has retained $33.25 in FICA and $90.00 in employees' income tax. Since the company is holding this money for the Internal Revenue Service—in effect, it owes this money to the Internal Revenue Service—these amounts represent *liabilities* of the company, and this *increase in liabilities* is shown by crediting two liability accounts—*FICA taxes payable* ($33.25) and *employee's federal income tax payable* ($90.00).

These debits and credits can be recorded in a combination journal. Note that total debits (salary expense) equal total credits (amount of cash paid plus amounts withheld and payable for taxes).

Combination Journal   Page 12

CASH DEBIT	CASH CREDIT	DATE	ACCOUNT	POST REF.	GENERAL DEBIT	GENERAL CREDIT	
	376 75	198— Mar 7	Salary Expenses		500 00		1
			F.I.C.A. tax payable			33 25	2
			Employees' Federal Income			90 00	3
			Tax Payable				4
							5

It is also possible to record payrolls and tax withholdings in a cash payments journal. This is done by providing special columns in which to record FICA tax payable credit and employee income tax payable credit.

Cash Payments Journal

DATE	CHECK NO.	ACCOUNT DEBIT	POST REF	GENERAL DEBIT	ACC. PAY DEBIT	SALARY EXP DEBIT	F I C A TAX PAYER CREDIT	FEDERAL INC TAX PAY. CR.	CASH CREDIT
198— Mar 7	355	Salary Expense				500 00	33 25	90 00	376 75

BOOKKEEPING ENTRIES FOR EMPLOYERS' PAYROLL TAXES

We have just seen above how the bookkeeping entries are made to record a payroll and the payroll taxes that are withheld from the *employees'* salaries. The *employer* must also pay his share of the FICA tax. These payments are an expense of the business. When these expenses are incurred, a journal entry is made to record the expense by *debiting an expense account called FICA tax.* When the expense is charged off, the business is in effect holding some monies that belong to the government, or to phrase it another way, the business owes these funds to the government. Therefore, a journal entry is made to record this liability *by crediting a liability account—FICA tax payable.*

For example, the Brown Manufacturing Company must pay the *employer's* FICA tax on its January 7th payroll recorded in the above payroll register. This will amount to 6.65% of the payroll, or $33.25. To record this, the bookkeeper *debits the expense account (FICA tax) and credits the liability account (FICA tax payable).*

Combination Journal

CASH DEBIT	CASH CREDIT		DATE	ACCOUNT	POST REF.	GENERAL DEBIT	GENERAL CREDIT
		1	198— Mar 7	F.I.C.A. Tax Expense		33 25	
		2		F.I.C.A. Tax Payable			33 25
		3					

The student will note that, after posting, the January 7th payroll has resulted in *two entries in the FICA tax payable account.* First of all, $33.25 was credited to the account as the *employees'* share of FICA taxes which were withheld from their paychecks. Then, an additional $33.25 was credited to the account as the *employer's* share.

F.I.C.A. Tax Payable   Account #25

DATE	ITEM	POST REF	DEBIT	DATE	ITEM	POST REF	DEBIT
198— Mar 7			33 25				
7			33 25				

Employers' unemployment taxes would be handled in the same way. For example, an expense account—state unemployment tax—would be debited for the amount of the tax, and a liability account—state unemployment tax payable—would be credited.

Combination Journal

CASH				DATE	ACCOUNT	POST REF.		
DEBIT	CREDIT							
			1	198— Mar 7	State Unemployment Tax Exp.		15 50	
			2		State Unemployment Tax Pay.			15 50
			3					
			4					

In some firms, the employer's payroll taxes are charged off at the time each payroll is prepared. In other firms, to save time, only one entry is made every three months for the liabilities incurred by the firm on all the payrolls written during the preceding three months.

PAYING WITHHELD FUNDS TO THE APPROPRIATE GOVERNMENT AGENCY

At various intervals the business is required to turn over to the appropriate government agency the taxes that it has withheld or set aside. To do this, the bookkeeper sends his bank or the Internal Revenue Service a check for an amount which includes the FICA taxes withheld from employees, and the amount contributed by the firm (as shown in the FICA taxes payable account), and also the federal income taxes withheld from employees (as shown in the employees federal income tax payable account). When this check is sent to the IRS, the firm's cash is decreased, so we *credit* the *cash account*. After the payment, the firm no longer owes the IRS FICA taxes payable or employees' federal income taxes payable, so *these two liability accounts* are debited to show the *decrease in liabilities*. These entries can be recorded in the combination journal or the general journal.

General Journal

CASH				DATE	ACCOUNTS	POST REF.	GENERAL	
DEBIT	CREDIT						DEBIT	CREDIT
	550 00		1	198— Apr 15	F.I.C.A. Tax Payable		100 00	
			2		Employees Fed. Inc. Tax Payable		450 00	
			3					
			4					
			5					

These entries showing payment to IRS of withheld funds could also be recorded in the cash payments journal.

Cash Payments Journal

	DATE	CHECK NO.	ACCOUNT DEBIT	POST REF.	GENERAL DEBIT	ACCTS. PAY DEBIT	CASH CREDIT
1	198— Apr. 15	75	F.I.C.A. Tax Payable		100 00		550 00
2			Employees Fed. Inc. Tax Payable		450 00		
3							

Payments of state or federal unemployment taxes withheld are handled in the same way. A check is sent to the appropriate government agency. The liability account—state unemployment taxes payable—is decreased (debited) and the cash account decreased (credited).

Chapter 25

Multiple Choice.

1. FICA tax is paid by _____

   a. employers only.
   b. employees only.
   c. both employers and employees.

2. Federal Income Tax_____

   a. by law must be withheld from employees' salaries as specified by IRS.
   b. may be withheld if employee requests it.
   c. is paid ½ by employee and ½ by employer.

3. When the information in the payroll register is journalized,_____

   a. the cash account is credited for the entire amount of monies earned by employees.
   b. the cash account is credited only for that amount of money actually paid employees.
   c. the cash account is always credited with the amount debited to the salary expense account.

4. When entering the *employer's* share of FICA taxes in the journal, the amount is debited to an expense account, and credited to_____

   a. an asset account.
   b. a liability account.
   c. an expense account.

5. When a check is sent to the bank or the Internal Revenue Service in payment of taxes previously withheld by a company, the cash account is credited and_____

   a. a liability account is reduced and debited.
   b. an asset account is debited.
   c. an expense account is debited.

6. The total amount of FICA taxes both withheld from employees and contributed by the firm during the preceding period and not as yet sent to IRS could be determined by consulting which ledger account?

   a. The FICA taxes payable account.
   b. The FICA tax expense account.
   c. The salary expense account.

7. To determine the total amount of the *employer's* FICA tax contribution during a period, the bookkeeper would consult which ledger account?

   a. The FICA taxes payable account.
   b. The FICA tax expense account.
   c. The cash account.

The Work Sheet: Adjustments | 26

THE ACCOUNTING CYCLE

Up to this point, we have seen the work of the book-keeper in connection with the recording of business transactions in the journals and ledgers. The entire process of recording business transactions and preparing summarized statements of the effects of these transactions is called the *accounting cycle* (or book-keeping cycle). It consists of several steps.

1. Business transaction occurs.
2. A business document is prepared as a result of the transaction (sales slip, credit memo, invoice, petty cash receipt, check, etc.).
3. Journal entries are made. The transaction may be journalized in a general or combination journal, or in one of the specialized journals (cash payments journal, etc.).
4. The journal is posted to the ledger. Some entries are posted first to a subsidiary ledger (accounts receivable ledger, etc.) and then, later on, totals are posted to the general ledger accounts.
5. At the end of the accounting period, a trial balance is prepared.

In the next few chapters we will study the last steps in the accounting cycle.

6. Adjusting and closing entries are prepared on the work sheet. These reflect changes in the ledger accounts that have occurred during the accounting period, but which have not yet been recorded in the ledger accounts at the time the trial balance is taken.
7. Work sheet is completed and financial statements are prepared from the work sheet.
8. Adjusting and closing entries are journalized and posted, and accounts in the ledger are closed, ruled or balanced as required.
9. Post-closing trial balance is taken.

THE WORK SHEET

The simplest method of organizing these last steps in the accounting cycle which are done at the end of the accounting period (usually at the end of the month) is through the use of a *work sheet*. A work

sheet is a single sheet of ruled analysis paper, with several columns in which various batches of figures can be entered. The work sheet is *not* part of the firm's permanent records as the journal and ledgers are, so it can be prepared in pencil.

1. **Form of the Work Sheet.** The work sheet is headed with the name of the firm, the title (work sheet), and the date. There are many different possible columnar arrangements. The one illustrated here is the 10-column work sheet.
2. **Recording Trial Balance.** The first step in preparing the work sheet is to copy the trial balance. Write the name and account number of each account in the trial balance on the work sheet, and copy the debit or credit balance for each account in the trial-balance debit (left) column or trial-balance credit (right) column. Draw a single line under the last entry. Total the two columns. Draw a double line under the totals.
3. **The Adjusting Entries.** One purpose of the work sheet is to simplify the preparation of the financial statements for the period (the profit and loss statement and the balance sheet). Often, it would be inaccurate to use the balances in the ledger accounts as shown in the trial balance to prepare these statements. This is because during the accounting period *various changes in the account balances have taken place that have not been recorded in the books.* These changes must now be recorded to bring the accounts up-to-date. These changes are called *adjustments* and the bookkeeping entries that record them are called *adjusting entries.*
   a. RECORDING ADJUSTMENTS IN THE WORK SHEET. The adjusting entries will eventually be journalized and posted in the ledger accounts. However, to simplify their preparation, they are first recorded in the adjustment debit (left) and adjustment credit (right) columns of the work sheet, and, later on, journalized and posted. Adjustments are similar to all other business transactions in that each adjustment results in equal debits and credits. Therefore, the student should

ACCOUNT NAME	ACCT #	TRIAL BALANCE DR.	CR.			
Cash	11	500				
Accounts Receivable	12	500				
Merchandise Inventory	13	400				
Supplies	14	100				
Accounts Payable	21		200			
R. Grace, Capital	31		1000			
R. Grace, Drawings	32	200				
Sales	41		2500			
Purchases	51	1000				
Salary Expense	52	400				
Rent Expense	53	400				
Misc. Expense	54	200				
		3700	3700			

R. Grace   Work Sheet   Month Ended Jan. 31, 198—

Copying Trial Balance To Worksheet

remember that each adjustment recorded in the work sheet must result in *equal entries* in the adjustment *debit* column and in the adjustment *credit* column.

b. KINDS OF ADJUSTMENTS.   There are various kinds of month-end adjustments that must be made. We will only discuss a few.

(1) Adjusting Merchandise Inventory. The balance in the ledger account for merchandise inventory shows the amount of inventory that was on hand at the beginning of the period. We know that this inventory has changed during the month as the company bought and sold merchandise. However, the balance in the account does not as yet reflect any of these changes.

(a) TAKING THE MERCHANDISE INVENTORY. An inventory or count of the merchandise on hand at the end of period must be taken. This is the *closing inventory* for the period.

(b) ADJUSTING THE BEGINNING INVENTORY FIGURE.   The beginning inventory figure is one of the expenses that goes into determining the profit and loss for the period. Therefore, we enter *beginning inventory* in the debit or left side of the adjustment column as a *debit to profit and loss summary account*. We enter the beginning inventory in the credit or right side of the adjustment column as a *credit to merchandise inventory*.

(c) ADJUSTING THE CLOSING INVENTORY FIGURE.   To show the amount of merchandise inventory now on hand at the end of the period, *debit the merchandise inventory account with the closing inventory.* (This figure has just been obtained by taking the inventory.) Credit this closing inventory to the profit and loss summary. Below we see how the closing inventory would be recorded and adjusting entries made. An inventory of merchandise was taken by R. Grace at the end of the period. It showed $300 worth of merchandise on hand. *The merchandise inventory account is debited with the amount of the closing inventory ($300) and the profit and loss summary is credited with the amount of the closing inventory ($300).* These adjusting entries are recorded in the adjustment columns.

R. Grace   Work Sheet   Month Ended Jan. 31, 198—

ACCOUNT NAME	ACCT #	TRIAL BALANCE DR.	TRIAL BALANCE CR.	ADJUSTMENT	
Cash	11	500			
Accounts Receivable	12	500			
Merchandise Inv.	13	400			400 (a)
Supplies	14	100			
Accounts Payable	21		200		
R. Grace, Capital	31		1000		
R. Grace, Drawing	32	200			
Sales	41		2500		
Purchases	51	1000			
Salary Expense	52	400			
Rent Expense	53	400			
Misc. Expense	54	200			
		3700	3700		
Profit and Loss Summary	33			400 (a)	

Adjusting For Beginning Inventory

R. Grace   Work Sheet   Month Ended Jan. 31, 198—

ACCOUNT NAME	ACCT #	TRIAL BALANCE DR.	TRIAL BALANCE CR.	ADJUSTMENTS		
Cash	11	500				
Accounts Receivable	12	500				
Merchandise Inv	13	400		300 (b)	400 (a)	
Supplies	14	100				
Accounts Payable	21		200			
R. Grace Capital	31		1000			
R. Grace Drawing	32	200				
Sales	41		2500			
Purchases	51	1000				
Salary Expense	52	400				
Rent Expense	52	400				
Misc Expense	54	200				
		3700	3700			
Profit and Loss Summary	33			400 (a)	300 (b)	

Adjusting For Closing Inventory

4. **Adjusting Supplies Account.** In the trial balance, the supplies account shows the amount of supplies on hand at the *beginning* of the period. During the period, however, some of these supplies have been used up, and we wish to make adjusting entries to show that these supplies have been used up and that there is now a different balance in the account.

a. TAKING SUPPLIES INVENTORY. An inventory or count is taken of the total amount of supplies now on hand.

b. DETERMINING AMOUNT OF SUPPLIES USED DURING THE PERIOD. The present amount of supplies is subtracted from the original amount as shown in the trial balance to determine how much of the supplies has been used during the period. For example, the supplies account had a balance of $100 at the beginning of the period as shown in the trial balance. An inventory shows $40 of supplies on hand at the close of the period. Therefore, $60 of supplies has been used during the period.

c. SHOWING ADJUSTMENT IN SUPPLIES. The supplies that have been used are an expense of the business and must be charged off to an expense account—supplies expense. *Debit the supplies expense account* with supplies used during the period, and *credit the supplies account.* We see this done below where entries are made in the adjustment column to record a debit of $60 to *supplies expense* (to show the expense) and a *credit* of $60 to *supplies account* (to show the reduction in the amount of supplies on hand).

d. PROVING THE ADJUSTMENT COLUMNS. Once all the necessary adjustments have been made, a line should be drawn under the adjustment debit and credit columns and the columns should be totaled. The total of the debit column should equal the total of the credit column. If so, a double line is drawn under the two columns.

5. **Adjusted Trial Balance Columns.** The next step is to draw up an adjusted trial balance in the next two columns of the work sheet, reflecting all the adjusting entries that have been made in the adjustment columns. Note how the adjusted trial balance column gives only the *net balance* ($300) for the merchandise inventory account and the net balance for the supplies account ($40). However, an exception is made for the profit and loss summary account—here *both the debit and the credit entries are copied over into the adjusted trial balance column.* This is done because both figures will be needed later on to prepare the profit and loss statement. Below we see the work sheet completed through the adjusted trial balance columns. Note how the adjustment columns and the adjusted trial balance columns have been totaled and ruled.

R. Grace   Work Sheet   Month Ended Jan 31, 198—

ACCOUNT NAME	ACCT #	TRIAL BALANCE DR.	TRIAL BALANCE CR.	ADJUSTMENTS	
Cash	11	500			
Accounts Receivable	12	500			
Merchandise Inv.	13	400		300 (b)	400 (a)
Supplies	14	100			60 (c)
Accounts Payable	21		200		
R. Grace Capital	31		1000		
R. Grace Drawing	32	200			
Sales	41		2500		
Purchases	51	1000			
Salary Expense	52	400			
Rent Expense	53	400			
Misc. Expense	54	200			
		3700	3700		
Profit and Loss Sum.	33			400 (a)	300 (a)
Supplies Expense	55			60 (c)	

Adjusting Supplies Account

R. Grace   Work Sheet   Month Ended Jan 31, 198—

ACCOUNT NAME	ACCT #	TRIAL BALANCE DR.	TRIAL BALANCE CR.	ADJUSTMENTS	ADJUSTMENTS	ADJUSTED TRIAL BALANCE DR.	ADJUSTED TRIAL BALANCE CR.
Cash	11	500				500	
Accounts Receivable	12	500				500	
Merchandise Inv	13	400		300 (b)	400 (a)	300	
Supplies	14	100			60 (c)	40	
Accounts Payable	21		200				200
R. Grace Capital	31		1000				1000
R. Grace Drawing	32	200				200	
Sales	41		2500				2500
Purchases	51	1000				1000	
Salary Expense	52	400				400	
Rent Expense	53	400				400	
Misc. Expense	54	200				200	
		3700	3700				
Profit and Loss Sum.	33			400 (a)	300 (b)	400	300
Supplies Expense	55			60 (c)		60	
				760	760	4000	4000

6. Profit and Loss Statement Columns and Balance Sheet Columns.

Each of the amounts in the adjusted trial balance columns is then copied into the debit or credit side of the profit and loss statement columns or into the debit or credit side of the balance sheet columns. If the account is an income or expense account, it is entered in the profit and loss columns. If it is an asset, liability or proprietorship account, it is entered in the balance sheet columns.

a. PROFIT AND LOSS STATEMENT COLUMNS. The fourth set of columns on the worksheet are the profit and loss statement columns. All the income accounts (sales, interest income, etc.) are copied into the profit and loss credit column. All the expense accounts (sales expense, rent expense, etc.) are copied into the profit and loss debit column. Both the debit and the credit entries in the *profit and loss summary account* are copied over into the profit and loss statement debit and credit columns.

A line is drawn under the profit and loss statement columns and the columns are totaled. *The difference between the income items in the credit column and the expense items in the debit column is the net profit for the period.* The amount of the profit is entered below the debit total in the debit column, and is called net profit. New totals are obtained for the two columns, and a double line is drawn.

In the profit and loss statement columns of the work sheet illustrated below, income items amounted to $2800 and expense items amounted to $2460. Therefore, net profit of $340 is entered in the debit column.

NOTE: If the *income items* entered in the credit side of the profit and loss column *were less than the expense items* on the debit side, then the firm would have a *net loss* for the period. The net loss would be entered in the credit column.

b. BALANCE SHEET COLUMNS. All the balance sheet accounts are then listed in the appropriate debit or credit sides of balance sheet columns of the work sheet. In addition to the regular balance sheet accounts already recorded, the amount of the net profit or loss is also copied into the balance sheet column. This net profit (or loss) represents an increase (or decrease) in the proprietorship

	ACCOUNT NAME	ACCT #	ADJUSTED TRIAL BALANCE		PROFIT AND LOSS STATEMENT	
1	Cash	11	500			
2	Accounts Receivable	12	500			
3	Merchandise Inv.	13	300			
4	Supplies	14	40			
5	Accounts Payable	21		200		
6	R Grace Capital	31		1000		
7	R Grace Drawing	32	200			
8	Sales	41		2500		2500
9	Purchases	51	1000		1000	
10	Salary Expense	52	400		400	
11	Rent Expense	53	400		400	
12	Misc. Expense	54	200		200	
13						
14	Profit and Loss Summary	33	400	300	400	300
15	Supplies Expense	55	60		60	
16			4000	4000	2460	2800
17	Net Profit				340	
18					2800	2800
19						
20						
21						
22						

Completing the Profit & Loss Statement Columns of the Worksheet

interest in the business, and as such is a balance sheet item. If a net profit has been earned, the net profit is entered as an increase in proprietorship (a credit) in the balance sheet columns. (A net loss represents a decrease in proprietorship, and as such, would be entered as a debit in the debit column of the balance sheet columns.) A line is then drawn under the two balance sheet columns; they are totaled and should be equal. A double line is then drawn.

Below we see the balance sheet columns from the R. Grace work sheet. Note that the net profit of $340 is entered as an increase in proprietorship on the credit side of the balance sheet columns.

ACCOUNT NAME	ACCT NO	ADJUSTED TRIAL BALANCE		PROFIT AND LOSS STATEMENT		BALANCE SHEET	
Cash	11	500				500	
Accts Receivable	12	500				500	
Merch Inven	13	300				300	
Supplies	14	40				40	
Accts Payable	21		200				200
R Grace Capital	31		1000				1000
R Grace Drawing	32	200				200	
Sales	41		2500		2500		
Purchase	51	1000		1000			
Salary Expense	52	400		400			
Rent Expense	53	400		400			
Merch Expense	54	200		200			
Profit and Loss Summary	33	400	300	400	300		
Supplies Expense	55	60		60			
		4000	4000	2460	2800		
Net Profit				340			340
				2800	2800	1540	1540

Completing the Balance Sheet Columns of the Work Sheet

Chapter 26

Multiple Choice.

1. The work sheet is_____

    a. part of the ledger.
    b. part of the journal.
    c. part of the firm's permanent records.
    d. not part of the firm's permanent records.

2. Month-end adjusting entries are made to_____

    a. correct wrong entries that have been posted to ledger accounts.
    b. close out income and expense accounts.
    c. reflect changes in account balances that have not as yet been recorded.

3. To adjust for beginning inventory, _____

    a. debit profit and loss summary and credit merchandise inventory.
    b. credit profit and loss summary and debit merchandise inventory.
    c. add purchases to closing inventory.

4. To adjust for closing inventory_____

    a. debit profit and loss summary and credit merchandise inventory.
    b. credit profit and loss summary and debit merchandise inventory.
    c. add purchases to closing inventory.

5. A firm had a beginning balance of $200 of mailroom supplies. No supplies were bought during the period. Closing inventory of supplies was $150. At the month end, the supplies expense account_____

    a. should be debited with $50.
    b. should be debited with $150.
    c. should be credited with $50.
    d. should be credited with $200.

6. In completing the profit and loss statement and balance sheet statement columns of the work sheet, net profit is_____

    a. listed only in the profit and loss statement columns.
    b. listed only in the balance sheet columns.
    c. not included in either profit and loss or balance sheet columns.
    d. included in both the profit and loss and balance sheet columns.

7. The accounting cycle (or bookkeeping cycle) consists of_____

    a. journalizing only.
    b. journalizing and posting only.
    c. preparing the work sheet only.
    d. all steps in recording business transactions, from the preparation of the original business document through the post closing trial balance.

Problems.

1. James Company's trial balance showed a beginning merchandise inventory of $5000. A physical inventory was taken at the end of the month and showed a closing inventory of $3500. What debit and credit entries should be made in the adjustment columns of the James Company's work sheet to adjust the inventory account?

   a. After these adjustments have been made, what balance will the merchandise inventory account show?

   b. How does this final balance in the merchandise inventory account compare with the actual amount of inventory on hand, as determined by the physical inventory that was taken?

2. The work sheet of the James Company lists the following accounts: cash, inventory, accounts payable, James Company capital, sales, miscellaneous expenses, profit and loss summary, net profit.

   a. What account balances should be listed in the profit and loss statement columns of the work sheet?

   b. Which account balances should be listed in the balance sheet statement columns of the work sheet?

3. Explain briefly how the profit and loss statement columns of the work sheet are used to determine the net profit or net loss for the period.

Financial Statements: The Profit and Loss Statement | 27

PURPOSE OF FINANCIAL STATEMENTS

Financial statements are prepared at the end of a given period—a month, a quarter of a year and/or a year. Financial statements *summarize the results* of all the business transactions which the bookkeeper has been recording during the period. Financial statements are used by several different groups who are concerned with the operations of the business.

1. **Owners.** The owner can use the summary of results of operations of the business in order to see how profitable his business has been, and to compare operations with the previous period.
2. **Creditors.** Banks and trade creditors (suppliers who grant the company credit) may wish to see financial statements in order to determine whether or not to advance credit to the business.
3. **Government.** Various state and federal government agencies require financial statements as a basis for determining tax liability.

PROFIT AND LOSS STATEMENT

The profit and loss statement (also called income statement) reports the amount of income the firm earned during the period, the expenses incurred, and the net profit or loss. The profit and loss state-

ment is prepared by using the figures given in the profit and loss columns of the work sheet.

NOTE: The profit and loss statement discussed directly below is for a *mercantile* firm, where most of the income is received from the sale of merchandise. Later on in the chapter, there is a discussion of a profit and loss statement for a business or profession which receives most of its income from fees for services rendered.

1. **Heading.** The heading of a profit and loss statement requires:
   a. Company's name.
   b. Title of this statement.
   c. Period of time covered by the statement.

For example, the profit and loss statement for R. Grace, whose work sheet was explained in the preceding chapter, would be headed as follows:

R. GRACE
Profit and Loss Statement
Month Ended January 31, 198—

2. **Income Section.** The first part of a profit and loss statement consists of a listing of all the income the company earned during the period. If we consult the profit and loss columns of the R. Grace work sheet,

Part of R Grace
Work Sheet
Month Ended Jan 31, 198—

		ACCOUNT NAME	ACCT. #	PROFIT AND LOSS STATEMENT	
1		Cash			
2		Accounts Receivable			
3		Merchandise Inv.			
4		Supplies			
5		Accounts Payable			
6		R Grace Drawing			
7		Sales			2500
8		Purchases		1000	
9		Salary Expense		400	
10		Rent Expense		400	
11		Misc. Expense		200	
12					
13		Profit and Loss Summary		400	300
14		Supplies Expense		60	
15				2460	2800
16		Net Profit		340	
17				2800	2800
18					

we see that the only income item was sales income—$2500. This is then listed as the first item on the profit and loss statement.

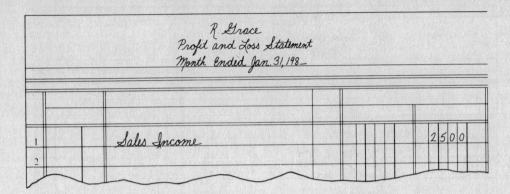

3. **Cost of Goods Sold.** When a business obtains most of its income from sale of merchandise, its expenses are divided into two groups—the actual *cost of the merchandise sold*, and all the other *expenses* involved in the business.

To obtain the cost of the goods sold, take the amount of goods that were on hand at the *beginning of the period*, and add all *purchases* made during the period.

These two items represent *the goods available for sale during the period*. To find the actual amount of goods sold, subtract the inventory of goods *left at the end of the period* (the closing inventory). The difference is called the *cost of goods sold*.

Beginning inventory
+ *Purchases*
Total cost of goods available for sale during the period,
− *Closing inventory*
Cost of goods sold

The *beginning inventory* figure is found in the profit and loss statement columns of the work sheet as a *debit to profit and loss summary*. *Purchases* are listed as a separate item. The *closing inventory* is found as a *credit to the profit and loss summary*. Thus, using the figures from the R. Grace work sheet profit and loss statement columns, the cost of goods sold section of the profit and loss statement is prepared.

1	Sales Income					2500
2	Cost of Goods Sold					
3	Beginning Merchandise Inventory Jan. 1			400		
4	Purchases			1000		
5	Total Cost of Mdse. Avail. for Sale			1400		
6	Closing Merchandise Inventory Jan. 31			300		
7	Cost of Goods Sold					1100
8						

R. Grace
Profit and Loss Statement
Month Ended Jan. 31, 198—

4. **Gross Profit on Sales.** The gross profit on sales is the difference between the income from sales and the cost of the merchandise sold. (Note that no *other expenses* aside from the actual cost of the goods sold are subtracted in determining the gross profit on sales.)

Income from sales
− Cost of goods sold
　Gross profit on sales.

In the case of R. Grace, sales income was $2500, cost of goods sold was $1100 and the gross profit on sales was $1400.

R. Grace
Profit and Loss Statement
Month Ended Jan. 31, 198—

1	Sales Income				2500
2	Cost of Goods Sold				
3	Beginning Merchandise Inventory Jan. 1		400		
4	Purchases		1000		
5	Total Cost of Mdse. Avail. for Sale		1400		
6	Closing Merchandise Inventory Jan. 31		300		
7	Cost of Goods Sold				1100
8	Gross Profit on Sales				1400
9					

5. Expenses. The next section of the profit and loss statement lists the expenses incurred by the firm *other* than the cost of goods sold. The list of expenses is obtained from the profit and loss statement columns of the work sheet. In the case of R. Grace, these expenses were

Selling expense	$400
Rent expense	400
Miscellaneous expense	200
Supplies expense	60
	$1060

6. Net Profit. These expenses are listed and totaled, and the total is subtracted from the gross profit on sales. The resulting figure is the net profit on sales for the business for the period.

Sales income
− Cost of goods sold
　Gross profit on sales
− Expenses
　Net profit on sales

In the case of R. Grace, gross profit on sales was $1400, expenses were $1060, and a net profit of $340 was earned.

R. Grace
Profit and Loss Statement
Month Ended Jan. 31, 198—

1	Sales Income				2500
2	Cost of Goods Sold:				
3	Beginning Merchandise Inventory Jan. 1		400		
4	Purchases		1000		
5	Total Cost of Merchandise for Sale		1400		
6	Closing Merchandise Inventory Jan. 31		300		
7	Cost of Goods Sold				1100
8	Gross Profit on Sale				1400
9	Expenses:				
10	Selling Expenses		400		
11	Rent Expense		400		
12	Miscellaneous Expense		200		
13	Supplies Expense		60		
14	Total Expenses				1060
15	Net Profit				340
16					
17					

In cases where the cost of goods sold plus expenses are *greater* than sales income, the company will have a net loss, rather than a net profit.

SERVICE BUSINESSES

Some businesses or professions obtain most of their income from fees for services or commissions, etc., rather than from selling merchandise (doctors, lawyers, rental agents, etc.). Businesses of this kind will not have a cost of goods sold section in their profit and loss statements, since what they are selling are services, *not* goods. For such operations, the profit and loss statement consists basically of a figure for income received from fees or commissions, an expense section, and a net profit (or loss) figure.

	John Devereaux Attorney-at-Law			
	Profit and Loss Statement			
	Year Ended Dec. 31, 198—			
1	Income from Fees			18300
2	Expenses:			
3	Rent Expense		2000	
4	Salary Expense		4000	
5	Misc. Expense		2000	
6	Total Expenses			8000
7	Net Profit			10300
8				

Chapter 27

1. What are the three items that are included in the heading of the profit and loss statement?

2. Below is a list of items found on the profit and loss statement.

   a. Sales income
   b. Net profit on sales
   c. Beginning inventory
   d. Expenses other than cost of goods sold
   e. Purchases
   f. Closing inventory
   g. Cost of goods sold
   h. Gross profit on sales

Using the above list, explain how each of the following amounts is determined.

   a. Cost of goods available for sale during the period.
   b. Cost of goods sold.
   c. Gross profit.
   d. Net profit.

3. Where on the work sheet does the bookkeeper find the following figures, which are needed to prepare the profit and loss statement?

    a. Beginning inventory.
    b. Closing inventory.
    c. Purchases.

4. During April, the Grepius Company had sales of $2000, a beginning inventory of $500, a closing inventory of $200, purchases of $600 and other expenses of $400.

    a. What was the cost of goods available for sale during April?
    b. What was the cost of goods sold during April?
    c. What was gross profit for April?
    d. What was net profit for April?

Financial Statements: The Balance Sheet | 28

BALANCE SHEET

Using the balance sheet statement columns of the work sheet, a balance sheet can be prepared.

HEADING

The balance sheet heading has three components:
1. **Name of Company.**
2. **Title of Statement—Balance Sheet.**
3. **Date of the Statement.** When the profit and loss statement was prepared, the heading showed the period of time covered in the statement—i.e., month ended Jan. 31st, or year ended Dec. 31st. The balance sheet, however, is a statement of the financial condition of the firm as of a single given date (not for an entire period). For example, the heading of the balance sheet for

R. Grace (prepared as a result of the worksheet given in an earlier chapter) would read:

R. GRACE
Balance Sheet
January 31, 198—

ASSET SECTION

The balances of all the asset accounts are listed and totaled. These balances are obtained from the left-hand balance sheet statement column of the worksheet.

LIABILITY SECTION

Next, the liability accounts and balances are listed and totaled.

Below, we see the balance sheet column section of the R. Grace work sheet for January 31, 198_, and the asset and liability sections of the balance sheet which have been prepared using the information in these columns.

R. Grace
Work Sheet
*Month Ended Jan. 31, 198_*

ACCOUNT NAME	Acct #	BALANCE	SHEET
Cash		500	
Accounts Receivable		500	
Merchandise Inventory		300	
Supplies		40	
Accounts Payable			200
R. Grace Capital			1000
R. Grace Drawing		200	
Sales			
Purchases			
Salary Expense			
Rent Expense			
Miscellaneous Expense			
Profit and Loss Summary			
Supplies Expense			
Net Profit			340
		1540	1540

R. Grace
Balance Sheet
*Jan. 31, 198_*

Assets			
Cash		500	
Accounts Receivable		500	
Merchandise Inventory		300	
Supplies		40	
Total Assets			1340
Liabilities			
Accounts Payable			200

PROPRIETORSHIP SECTION

The proprietorship section of the balance sheet must show:

1. Balance in the *capital account.*
2. Withdrawals made by the proprietor during the period (balance in the *drawing* account).
3. Additions or decreases in proprietorship due to net profit or net loss for the period (balance in the *net profit* or net loss for the period account).

Using the information in the work sheet, the following proprietorship section can be prepared for R. Grace January 31st balance sheet.

	PROPRIETORSHIP			
1	R. Grace, Capital		1000	
2	Net Profit for January	340		
3	Less: Withdrawals	200		
4	Net Increase in Capital		140	
5	R. Grace, Present Capital			1140
6				

If R. Grace had withdrawn more during the month than his net profit, there would have been a *net decrease* in the proprietorship. For example, assume he had withdrawn $500 during the month (as shown by a $500 balance in the drawing account), and that the net profit for the period has been $300. In such a case, the proprietorship section of the balance sheet would show a decrease of $200.

	PROPRIETORSHIP			
1	R. Grace, Capital		1000	
2	Withdrawals	500		
3	Less: Net Profit for Jan.	300		
4	Net Decrease in Capital		200	
5	R. Grace, Present Capital			800
6				

The complete balance sheet can be presented either in the *report* form, with items listed one under the other, or in the *account* form, with assets listed on the left side, and liabilities and proprietorship listed on the right side.

R. Grace
Balance Sheet
Jan. 31, 198—

Assets				
Cash		500		
Accounts Receivable		500		
Merchandise Inventory		300		
Supplies		40		
Total Assets			1340	
Liabilities				
Accounts Payable			200	
Proprietorship				
R. Grace, Capital		1000		
Net Profit – Jan.	340			
Less Withdrawals	200			
Net Increase in Capital		140		
R. Grace, Present Capital				1140
Total Liab. and Prop.				1340

Report Form of Balance Sheet

R. Grace
Balance Sheet
Jan. 31, 198—

Assets			Liabilities			
Cash		500	Accounts Payable			200
Accounts Receivable		500				
Merchandise Inventory		300	Proprietorship			
Supplies		40	R. Grace, Capital	1000		
			Net Profit	340		
			Less Withdrawals	200		
			Net Increase in Prop.		140	
			R. Grace Present Capital			1140
Total Assets		1340	Total Liabilities and Prop.			1340

Account Form of Balance Sheet

Chapter 28

1. What are the three components of the heading of the balance sheet?
2. Is the date expressed in the same way in the heading of the profit and loss statement as it is in the heading of the balance sheet? Why?
3. The proprietorship section of the balance sheet frequently shows the withdrawals that the proprietor has made during the period. From which source is this figure obtained by the bookkeeper in preparing the balance sheet?
4. Do withdrawals increase or decrease the balance in the proprietorship account? Do profits increase or decrease the proprietorship account? Do losses increase or decrease the proprietorship account?
5. At the end of April, James Richard's worksheet showed a capital account with a credit balance of $5000, a drawing account with a debit balance of $1000 and net profit for the period of $2000. What was his total present capital at the end of April?

Adjusting and Closing Entries | 29

ADJUSTMENTS

We saw in Chapter 26 how various adjustments had to be made to the balances in certain ledger accounts after the trial balance was taken. These adjustments were necessary to reflect the changes that had actually taken place in the account balances, but which had not been recorded during the month. Adjustments were made to merchandise inventory account to reflect the physical inventory of merchandise on hand at the months end. Adjustments were also made to the supplies accounts to reflect the supplies that were used during the month. These adjustments were made directly on the worksheet. It is necessary, however, to record the adjustments in the journals and ledger of the firm.

ADJUSTING ENTRIES

Adjusting entries are recorded in the general journal of the firm. Usually, the entire month-end group of adjusting entries is recorded in the journal at one time. These entries may be identified as adjusting entries by writing the words "adjusting entries" in the journal in the center of the line above the first adjusting entry.

USING THE WORK SHEET AS THE SOURCE OF THE ADJUSTING ENTRIES

The adjusting entries may be copied into the journal from the adjustment column of the work sheet. Below are found the adjustment columns of the R. Grace work sheet, from which all the adjusting entries discussed in this chapter have been prepared.

R. Grace
Work Sheet
Month Ended Jan. 31, 198—

					ADJUSTMENTS	
1	Cash					
2	Accounts Receivable					
3	Merchandise Inventory				300	400
4	Supplies					60
5	Accounts Payable					
6	R. Grace, Capital					
7	R. Grace, Drawing					
8	Sales					
9	Purchases					
10	Salary Expense					
11	Rent Expense					
12	Misc. Expense					
13						
14	Profit and Loss Summary				400	300
15	Supplies Expense				60	
16					760	760

1. Adjusting Entries for Beginning Inventory. The adjustments columns of the work sheet show that a credit to merchandise inventory of $400 and a debit to profit and loss summary of $400 were made to adjust for the beginning inventory. (See Chapter 26 for discussion of adjustments if you are not clear on why this was done.) These debits and credits are now recorded in a set of journal entries.

DATE		ACCOUNT	POST REF.	DEBIT	CREDIT
198— Jan.	31	Adjusting Entries Profit and Loss Summary		400	
		Merchandise Inventory			400

General Journal — Page 7

2. Adjusting Entries for Closing Inventory. The adjustments columns of the R. Grace work sheet show that a debit to merchandise inventory of $300 and a credit to profit and loss summary of $300 were made to adjust for the closing inventory. These debits and credits are now recorded in a set of journal entries.

DATE		ACCOUNT	POST REF.	DEBIT	CREDIT
198— Jan.	31	Merchandise Inventory		300	
		Profit and Loss Summary			300

General Journal — Page 7

3. Adjusting Entries for Supplies. The adjustments columns of the work sheet show a credit of $60 to supplies and a debit of $60 to supplies expense. These adjustments were made to reflect supplies used during the period. These debits and credits are now recorded in a set of journal entries.

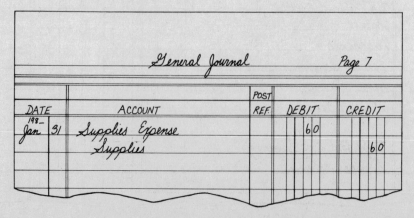

DATE		ACCOUNT	POST REF.	DEBIT	CREDIT
198— Jan.	31	Supplies Expense		60	
		Supplies			60

General Journal — Page 7

POSTING THE ADJUSTING ENTRIES

After the adjusting entries have been made in the journal, they are posted in the usual fashion to the ledger accounts. Here we see the section of the journal in which all the adjusting entries were journalized, and the ledger accounts into which the journal entries were then posted.

General Journal   Page 7

DATE		ACCOUNT	POST REF.	DEBIT	CREDIT
		Adjusting Entries			
198– Jan	31	Profit and Loss Summary		4 00	
		Merchandise Inv.			4 00
	31	Merchandise Inventory		3 00	
		Profit and Loss Summary			3 00
	31	Supplies Expense		60	
		Supplies			60

Profit and Loss Summary   Acct. #33

DATE		ITEM	POST REF.	DEBIT	DATE		ITEM	POST REF.	CREDIT
198– Jan	31		7	4 00 00	198– Jan	31		7	3 00 00

Merchandise Inventory   Acct. #13

DATE		ITEM	POST REF.	DEBIT	DATE		ITEM	POST REF.	CREDIT
198– Jan	1	Balance	1	4 00 00	198– Jan	31		7	4 00 00
	31		7	3 00 00					

Supplies   Acct. #14

DATE		ITEM	POST REF.	DEBIT	DATE		ITEM	POST REF.	CREDIT
198– Jan	1	Balance	1	1 00 00	198– Jan	31		7	60 00

DATE	ITEM	POST REF	DEBIT	DATE	ITEM	POST REF	CREDIT
199– Jan. 31		7	60 00				

Supplies Expense — *acct. #55*

Note that the merchandise inventory and supplies accounts show a balance as of Jan. 1st. This was the beginning inventory and the beginning amount of supplies on hand at the beginning of the month.

CLOSING ENTRIES

At the end of the accounting period, *all expense and revenue accounts, and most drawing accounts are closed.* This means that their balances are transferred into the permanent proprietorship account. After this has been done, the permanent proprietorship capital account will reflect all the increases and decreases which have taken place in the proprietorship interest in the business during the period, from profits, losses and withdrawals, and expense, revenue and drawing accounts that have been closed will have no balances.

1. **Closing an Income Account.** There are several kinds of closing entries. Income accounts are closed by transferring their balances to the profit and loss summary account. Since income accounts normally have credit balances, this is done by *debiting the income account with the amount of its balance and the crediting profit and loss summary.* For example, we knew from the R. Grace work sheet that the sales income account has a credit balance of $2500, at the month's end.

Sales Income
	$2500

To close the account, debit it with $2500,[a] and credit profit and loss summary with $2500.[a]

Sales Income		**Profit & Loss Summary**	
(a) $2500	$2500	(a) $2500	

This transaction would be journalized in the general journal, as the first of the entire group of closing entries that will be journalized. Frequently, the entire group of closing entries is so identified in the journal by writing this phrase "closing entries" in the center of the next line in the journal.

General Journal — *Page 7*

	DATE		ITEM	POST REF.	DEBIT	CREDIT
1			Closing Entries			
2	198– Jan.	31	Sales Income		25 00	
3			Profit and Loss Summary			25 00
4						

2. **Closing an Expense Account.** Expense accounts are closed by transferring the balance to the profit and loss summary. Since expense accounts normally have debit balances, this is done by *crediting the expense account with the amount of its balance, and debiting the profit and loss summary.* For example, we know from the R. Grace work sheet that the salary expense account has a debit balance of $400.

Salary Expense
$400	

This account is closed by crediting salary expense with $400[b], and debiting profit and loss summary with $400[b].

Salary Expense	Profit & Loss Summary
$400 | $400 (b)	(b) $400 |

In a similar way, all the other expense accounts would be closed into the profit and loss summary. Here we see a section of the R. Grace journal recording all the closing entries for expense accounts. Since all the expense account closings involve a debit to profit and loss summary, individual credit entries are made for each expense account, but only one debit entry (the total) is made to profit and loss summary.

	DATE		ACCOUNT TITLE	POST REF.	DEBIT	CREDIT
1	198— Jan	31	Profit and Loan Summary		20 60	
2			Salary Expense			4 00
3			Rent Expense			4 00
4			Miscellaneous Expense			2 00
5			Supplies Expense			60
6			Purchases			10 00

General Journal — Page 7

3. Closing Profit and Loss Summary Account.

We have seen how all the income and expense accounts have been closed out into the profit and loss summary account. The balance in each *income* account is credited to the profit and loss summary; the balance in each *expense* account is *debited* to the profit and loss summary. In addition, we saw earlier in this chapter (under adjusting entries) how the beginning balance in the merchandise inventory account was credited to the profit and loss summary and how the closing balance in the merchandise inventory account was debited to the profit and loss summary.

Profit & Loss Summary Account

Debits	*Credits*
1. balances in expense accounts	1. balances in income account
2. closing merchandise inventory	2. beginning merchandising inventory

Once all of these entries have been journalized and posted to the profit and loss summary account, the account is totaled and the balance determined. Then *the profit and loss summary account itself is closed by transferring its balance to the proprietor's drawing account.* If the firm has a profit, there will be a credit balance in the profit and loss summary account, and this is transferred by *debiting the profit and loss summary account for the amount of the balance and crediting the proprietor's drawing account.*

After all the adjusting and closing entries had been journalized and posted for R. Grace, its profit and loss summary account was totaled and the balance determined. A credit balance of $340 was found by subtracting the total debits from the total credits ($2800 less $2460 equals $340).

113

					Profit and Loss Summary			Acct. #33

DATE		ITEM	POST REF.	DEBIT	DATE		ITEM	POST REF.	CREDIT
198— Jan.	31		7	4 00	198— Jan.	31		7	3 00
	31		7	20 60		31		7	25 00

The account was then closed by debiting it with $340 and crediting R. Grace, drawing, for $340, as shown in the following journal entry.

		General Journal			Page 7

DATE		ACCOUNT	POST REF.	DEBIT	CREDIT
198— Jan.	31	Profit and Loss Summary	33	3 40	
		R. Grace, Drawing	32		3 40

This journal entry is then posted to the profit and loss summary account.

					Profit and Loss Summary			Acct. #33

DATE		ITEM	POST REF.	DEBIT	DATE		ITEM	POST REF.	CREDIT
198— Jan.	31		7	4 00	198— Jan.	31		7	3 00
	31		7	20 60		31		7	25 00
	31		7	3 40					

4. Closing the Drawing Account. If the proprietor wishes to withdraw the balance in the drawing account in the near future, he will leave the balance in that account. If, however, he wishes to keep the balance in the business permanently, as part of the permanent capital of the business, he will show this by *transferring the balance from the drawing account to* *the permanent capital account.* This is done by debiting the drawing account for the amount of the balance, and crediting the capital account. We see below the R. Grace drawing account after the $340 balance in the profit and loss summary account has been transferred to the drawing account.

DATE		ITEM	POST REF	DEBIT	DATE		ITEM	POST REF	CREDIT
R. Grace, Drawing									Acct. #32
198—Jan	15			1 0 0	198—Jan	31			3 4 0
	30			1 0 0					

The drawing account has a credit balance of $140. Mr. Grace decides to keep this as part of the permanent capital of the business, so he closes the drawing account into the permanent capital account. This is done by debiting the drawing account with $140 and crediting R. Grace, capital account with $140. The following journal entries are made to record this transfer.

General Journal   Page 7

	DATE		ACCOUNT	POST REF.	DEBIT	CREDIT
1	198—Jan	31	R. Grace, Drawing		1 4 0	
2			R. Grace, Capital			1 4 0
3						

5. **Summary.** All the month-end closing entries are shown graphically in the following illustration. This illustration assumes that a profit was earned, and that the profit exceeded drawings by the proprietor during the period.

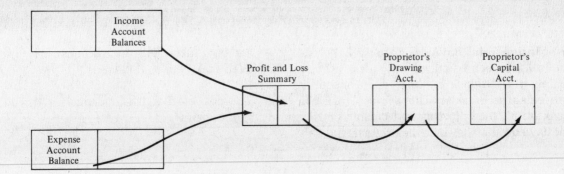

RULING AND BALANCING THE LEDGER

After all the adjusting and closing entries have been journalized and posted, the ledger is ruled and balanced.

1. **Income, Expense and Other Closed Accounts.** We have seen above that all income and expense accounts are *closed* at the month's end, and that certain other accounts, such as the profit and loss summary and the drawing account are closed too. To show that the accounts have been closed and *have no balances at the month's end* draw a single line under the last figure in the longer of the two columns and on the same line of the shorter column. Write the total of each column beneath this line. Both sides will have the same total, since the account has been closed. A double line is drawn across all the columns except the item column.

115

DATE		ITEM	POST REF.	DEBIT	DATE		ITEM	POST REF.	CREDIT
198– Jan	1		2	1 00	198– Jan	31		J7	4 00
	15		3	1 50					
	29		5	1 50					
				4 00					4 00

General ledger salary expense account closed and ruled

2. Asset Liability and Open Proprietorship Accounts.

The asset, liability and some proprietorship accounts will probably have balances and remain open at the months end. The balance in each of these accounts has been obtained previously by footing and balancing as explained in Chapter 7. The balance is entered on the appropriate side of the account. A single line is drawn. Both sides of the account are totaled. A double line is drawn under all the columns except the item column. The opening date of the new period is written on the next line under the double line and the balance is entered as the opening entry for the new period. A check is placed in the post. ref. column to show that this entry is an opening balance and not a posting from the journal.

Cash — acct. #1

DATE		ITEM	POST REF.	DEBIT	DATE		ITEM	POST REF.	CREDIT
198– Jan	1	Balance	✓	7 00	198– Jan	31		CP2	8 00
	31		CP4	6 00		31	Balance	✓	5 00
				13 00					13 00
198– Feb	1	Balance	✓	5 00					

General ledger open account, showing the account totaled and ruled,
and the new balance for the new period entered.

3. Post-Closing Trial Balance.

After all the accounts have been balanced and ruled, a *post-closing trial balance* of those open accounts with balances is taken. This serves as a final check on all the adjusting and closing entries that have been made since the original trial balance was taken. The same procedure is followed as in making a trial balance.

The post-closing trial balance for R. Grace is shown below.

R. GRACE
Post-Closing Trial Balance
Jan 31, 198—

Cash	500	
Accounts Receivable	500	
Merchandise Inventory	300	
Supplies	40	
Accounts Payable		200
R. Grace, Capital		1140
	1340	1340

Chapter 29

True or False.

1. Adjusting entries are recorded only on the worksheet and not in the journals or ledgers.
2. To adjust for beginning inventory, debit the profit and loss summary account and the credit merchandise inventory.
3. Adjusting entries are journalized into the specialized journals of the firm.
4. At the month's end, income accounts are closed out into the cash accounts.
5. All expense accounts are closed out into the profit and loss summary account.
6. When ledger accounts are closed at the end of the period, the profit and loss summary account is debited with the balances in the expense accounts.
7. When ledger accounts are closed at the end of the period, the profit and loss summary account is credited with the balances in the sales income accounts.
8. The asset and liability accounts are closed at the end of the accounting period and their balances are transferred to the profit and loss summary account.
9. The profit and loss summary account is closed out into the cash account.
10. After all expense and income accounts have been closed out into the profit and loss summary account, a net *debit* balance in that account means that the firm has a *profit* on operations for the period.
11. The profit and loss summary account is usually closed out by transferring its balance to the drawing account.
12. If the proprietor plans to keep net profits for the period as part of the permanent capital of the firm, the drawing account should be closed out into the permanent capital account.
13. All ledger accounts are closed at the end of the accounting period and have no balances.
14. Most expense and income account balances that appear in the trial balance will also appear in the post-closing trial balance.

ANSWERS TO TEST YOURSELF EXAMINATIONS

CHAPTERS 1 TO 5:

1. Asset	6. Asset
2. Asset	7. Asset
3. Liability	8. Proprietorship
4. Liability	9. Asset
5. Liability	10. Asset

1. a	6. d
2. d	7. c
3. d	8. b
4. d	9. c
5. a	10. a

1. Debit	9. Crediting
2. Debit	10. Debited
3. Debiting	11. Credited
4. Credit	12. Credited
5. Credit	13. Credited, debited
6. Credit	14. Decreased
7. Crediting	15. Debited, credited
8. Crediting	16. Increased, debiting

1. A capital account is another name for a proprietorship account, showing the ownership interest in the assets.
2. The debit side of an account is the left-hand side.
3. A liability account is a listing of a class or group of debts owed.
4. The fundamental accounting equation: Assets = liabilities + proprietorship.
5. A balance sheet is a listing of assets on the left, and claims against these assets—proprietorship and liabilities—on the right.

CHAPTERS 6 AND 7:

1. False	10. True
2. False	11. True
3. True	12. True
4. True	13. False
5. False	14. False
6. False	15. True
7. False	16. True
8. True	17. True
9. False	18. False

1. *Trial balance* is a listing of account debit balances in one column and account credit balances in another. If they are equal, the trial balance is said to be in balance.

2. *Balancing an account* involves subtracting the lower of the debit and credit footings from the higher, and writing the answer in small pencil numbers on the higher side.
3. *Footing an account* involves adding up the debit and credit sides of the account.
4. *Chart of accounts* is a listing of the number of each account in the ledger.
5. *"Out of balance"* trial balance means that the debit balances do not equal the credit balances.
6. The *ledger* is a group of accounts usually kept in a file or loose-leaf book.

CHAPTER 8:

1. False	6. False
2. False	7. True
3. True	8. True
4. True	9. False
5. True	10. True

1. *Journalizing* is the process of recording transactions in the journal.
2. *A book of original entry* is a bookkeeping record in which the first entry of a transaction is recorded. The journal is a book of original entry.
3. *A compound journal entry* is a journal entry involving more than one debit and/or credit entry for a single transaction.
4. The process of copying debits and credits from the journal into the individual ledger accounts is called *posting*.
5. The journal page number in the ledger account post. ref. column is a *post mark*. The ledger account number in the post. ref. column of the journal is also a *post mark*.

1. It is difficult to retrace a transaction if entered directly in the ledger accounts, since each half of the transaction is in a different place.

   There is no chronological record of all the transactions of a firm unless a journal is used.

   It is difficult to find errors if direct ledger accounting is used.

2. The bookkeeper enters the number of the ledger account to which each journal entry is posted, in the post. ref. column of the journal. Therefore, at any time, she can look at the post. ref. column of the journal to find where she posted the entry.

Similarly, the journal page number is posted in the ledger account when an entry is posted. At any future time the bookkeeper can determine the page of the journal from which the ledger entry came, simply by consulting the post. ref. column of the ledger.

CHAPTER 9:

1. Only one line is required for journalizing a cash transaction.
2. Two lines are required for journalizing non-cash transactions.
3. No. Entries in the cash debit and cash credit columns are posted individually to the cash account. Instead, at the month's end, the totals of the cash columns are posted to the cash account.
4. Each entry in the general debit and general credit column is posted individually to its appropriate ledger account.
5. The totals of the cash credit and cash debit columns are posted at the month end as debits and credits to the ledger cash account.
6. The totals of the general credit and general debit columns are not posted. During the month, each individual item entered in a general credit or general debit column has been posted individually to a ledger account. Therefore, there is no need to post the total of the column.
7. The total of this additional "special column" would also be posted at the month's end, at the same time the other special columns (cash debit and cash credit) were posted.

CHAPTER 10:

1. True		8. False
2. False		9. False
3. False		10. True
4. True		11. True
5. True		12. True
6. True		13. True
7. True		14. False

CHAPTER 11:

1. a		6. b
2. b		7. b
3. d		8. b
4. b		9. c
5. a		10. c

CHAPTER 13:

1. True		7. True
2. False		8. False
3. False		9. True
4. True		10. False
5. False		11. True
6. True		

CHAPTER 19:

1. A credit memo is a business document or form issued to a customer when he returns goods or is permitted an allowance. This form is used as the basis for crediting the amount of the return or the allowance to the customer's account in the accounts receivable ledger.
2. A sales allowance is a reduction in cost granted a customer without requiring actual physical return of the merchandise.
3. The sales returns and allowances account is a ledger account to which all returns or allowances permitted customers are debited.
4. The purchase returns and allowances journal is a special journal in which all transactions involving returns or allowances on merchandise *purchased* by the firm are journalized.

   1. Debit sales returns and allowances. Credit cash.
   2. Debit sales returns and allowances. Credit Jones' account in accounts receivable ledger.
   3. Debit Happy Boot account in accounts payable ledger. Credit purchases returns and allowances.
   4. Debit Green Jacket Corp. account in accounts payable ledger. Credit purchases returns and allowances.
   5. Debit sales returns and allowances. Credit Sandra Smith's account in accounts receivable ledger.

CHAPTER 20:

1. False		6. True
2. False		7. False
3. True		8. True
4. False		9. True
5. False		10. True

1. Debit cash $98 and sales discount $2. Credit customer's account $100.
2. Debit cash $100. Credit customer's account $100.
3. Debit creditor's account $500. Credit cash $495 and purchase discount $5.
4. Debit creditor's account $500. Credit cash $500.

CHAPTER 21:

1. A promissory note is an unconditional promise in writing made by one party to pay a stated amount of money to another party either on demand, or on a specific date.
2. The person who signs the promissory note (and promises to pay the money) is the maker of the note.
3. A promissory note is negotiable since it can be transferred or sold to a third party before it is due.
4. When a promissory note is transferred to a third party, it must be signed on the back by the payee (the person to whom it is payable). This is called endorsing the note.
5. Notes payable are liabilities consisting of promissory notes made out to others.

6. Notes receivable are assets consisting of promissory notes payable to the holder.

1. Debit notes receivable, credit Cynthia Hardware account in accounts receivable ledger.

2. Debit cash, credit notes receivable.
3. Debit cash, credit notes payable.
4. Debit US Steel account in accounts payable ledger, credit notes payable.
5. Debit notes payable, credit cash.

Combination Journal — Page 25

DATE	ITEM	POST REF	CASH DEBIT	CASH CREDIT	GENERAL DEBIT	GENERAL CREDIT	ACCOUNTS RECEIV DEBIT	ACCOUNTS RECEIV CREDIT	SALES DISCOUNT DEBIT	ACCOUNTS PAYABLE DEBIT	ACCOUNTS PAYABLE CREDIT	PURCHASE DISCOUNT CREDIT
198— 1	Sales Returns & All				100 00							
	Arthur Jay							100 00				
2	Sales Returns & All			50 00	50 00							
3	Harris Supply									50 00		
	Purch. Return & All					50 00						
6	Harris Supply			98 00						100 00		2 00
7	Richard Smith		196 00					200 00	4 00			
8	Arthur Jay		50 00					50 00				
9	Sales Returns & All				40 00							
	Jim Green							40 00				
10	Notes Payable		1000 00			1000 00						
13	Notes Receivable				75 00							
	Gladys Smith							75 00				
15	Notes Recevable		100 00			100 00						
16	Notes Payable			500 00	500 00							
19	Purchases				1000 00							
	Soap Superior										1000 00	

CHAPTER 22:

1. Debit notes receivable $1000. Credit sales $1000.
2. Debit cash $1015. Credit notes receivable $1000. Credit interest income $15.
3. Debit notes receivable $500. Credit accounts receivable $500.
4. Debit cash $50. Credit notes receivable $50.
5. Debit notes payable $2000. Debit interest expense $50. Credit cash $2050.
6. Debit notes payable $500. Credit cash $500.
7. Debit cash $1020. Credit notes receivable $1000. Credit interest income $20.

CHAPTER 23:

1. *Bank signature card.* This is a card signed by each person authorized to sign checks for a company. A bank requires that such a signature card be filled out when an account is opened. The bank keeps the signature card.
2. *Endorsement in full.* Endorsement in full appears on the back of check and reads "for deposit in account of_____" and is signed by the person to whom the check is made out. Every check must be endorsed before it can be deposited. An endorsement in full protects the depositor, since the check can be deposited only in the account indicated in the endorsement.
3. *Deposit slip.* A deposit slip is a form listing all the currency, checks, etc. that are being deposited in the bank. A deposit slip usually accompanies each bank deposit.
4. *Cancelled checks.* Cancelled checks are those that were written by a depositor, cashed (presented for payment) by the person to whom they were made out, and paid by the bank. Cancelled checks are returned each month to the depositor along with his bank statement.
5. *Outstanding checks.* Outstanding checks are those which have been written and sent out, but which have not yet been presented for payment at the bank.

Problem:

Balance in check-book	$600	Balance in bank statement	$580
Deduct: Service charge	5	Deduct: Outstanding check	10
	$595		$570
		Add: Unrecorded deposit	25
Corrected check-book balance	$595	Corrected bank statement balance	$595

CHAPTER 24:

1. True
2. False
3. True
4. True
5. False
6. False
7. True
8. False
9. True
10. True
11. False

CHAPTER 25:

1. c
2. a
3. b
4. b

5. a
6. a (Note that FICA Tax expense account only includes *employer's* contribution.)
7. b

CHAPTER 26:

1. d
2. c
3. a
4. b

5. a
6. d
7. d

1. a. debit profit and loss summary $5000
   credit merchandise inventory $5000
   debit merchandise inventory $3500
   credit profit and loss summary $3500
   b. $3500
   c. The balance as shown in the merchandise inventory account agrees with the balance as shown by the physical inventory

2. a. sales, misc. expense, profit and loss summary and net profit
   b. cash, inventory, accounts payable, James Co. capital, net profit

3. The balances in the right-hand or credit column are totaled, and the balances in the left-hand or debit column are totaled. If credit balances exceed debit balances, the difference is the net profit for the period. If debit balances exceed credit balances, the difference is the net loss for the period.

CHAPTER 27:

1. Name of company, title of statement (profit and loss statement), period of time covered by the statement (i.e., month ended November 30, 198—).

2. c. and e. Beginning inventory plus purchases.
   c., e. and f. Beginning inventory plus purchases minus closing inventory.

a. and g. Sales income less cost of goods sold.
d. and h. Gross profit less other expenses.

3. a. These figures would be found in profit and loss statement columns as a debit to profit and loss summary.
   b. These figures would be found in profit and loss statement columns as a credit to profit and loss summary.
   c. Purchases can be obtained by using the figure for purchases as shown in the profit and loss statement columns of the work sheet.

4. a. $500 + $600 = $1100.
   b. $500 + $600 − $200 = $900.
   c. $2000 − $900 = $1100.
   d. $1100 − $400 = $700.

CHAPTER 28:

1. Name of firm, date as of which the balance sheet is prepared, and title of the financial statement (balance sheet).

2. No. The profit and loss statement reports operating results for an entire period, whereas the balance sheet reports the financial condition as of a given date. Therefore, the profit and loss statement date will be for an entire month, or quarter or year, whereas the balance sheet date will be for a single date.

3. Withdrawals are obtained from the debit balance of the drawing account.

4. Withdrawals decrease proprietorship. Profits increase it and losses decrease it.

5. Total month-end capital would be original capital ($5000) less withdrawals ($1000), plus profits ($2000), or $6000 in all.

CHAPTER 29:

1. False
2. True
3. False
4. False
5. True
6. True
7. True

8. False
9. False
10. False
11. True
12. True
13. False
14. False